FRANCIS HUTCHESON AND DAVID HUME
AS PREDECESSORS OF ADAM SMITH

FRANCIS HUTCHESON AND DAVID HUME AS PREDECESSORS OF ADAM SMITH

W. L. TAYLOR

Professor of Economics
in the University College
of Rhodesia and Nyasaland

DUKE UNIVERSITY PRESS

Durham, North Carolina

1965

© 1965, Duke University Press

Library of Congress Catalogue Card number 65-20591

Printed in the United States of America by
Kingsport Press, Inc., Kingsport, Tennessee

To ELIZABETH

For a Pilgrimage Shared

PREFACE

This book is the outcome of work in widely separate years and places. It was fourteen years ago at the University of Otago, New Zealand, that I first became interested in the contributions to the development of economic thought of some of the eighteenth-century Scottish philosophers. It was Dr. H. Bernardelli, now of the University of Auckland, who first introduced me to this field with his superbly iconoclastic teaching of doctrinal history. Two years later I was privileged to go to the London School of Economics, where in the summer of 1954 the basic research for the study was completed. This period was distinguished by the friendly guidance and encouragement I received from Professor T. W. Hutchison. Later that year I joined the staff of the University of Cape Town, where my interest in the field was enlivened and nurtured by Professor H. M. Robertson, whose impeccable scholarship and gentle understanding did much to encourage me.

At the end of 1956 I went to the newly established University College of Rhodesia and Nyasaland as a foundation member of the staff. Paradoxically, this meant nearly six years' suspension of my work in this field. The economic problems, political tensions, and difficulties associated with the Federation of Rhodesia and Nyasaland, together with the heavy burden of developing a new Department of Economics in a new university with all the attendant administrative erosion of one's time, saturated most of the waking hours of my life. Certainly eighteenth-century political economy was far removed from the immediate realities of academic life and day-to-day living in that turbulent period of Central Africa's history. Constitutions and conferences, capital-output ratios and the subsistence and cash economies—the wealth of the nation—rather than the niceties of the water-diamond paradox, and the fun of the "private vice—publick benefit" debates, absorbed my time.

An invitation in the summer of 1963 to return to the University of Otago during my sabbatical leave from the University College of Rhodesia and Nyasaland afforded me an ideal opportunity to return to the subject of my earlier work. It was apt that this work should be prepared for publication where it had its beginning almost a decade and a half ago.

By means of quotations and references I have tried to make clear my indebtedness to other writers. To the very fine original scholarship of Edwin Cannan, C. R. Fay, James Bonar, and W. R. Scott I am indebted in ways impossible to identify. I wish, however, to mention particularly the very valuable advice I have had from Professor T. W. Hutchison and Professor H. M. Robertson, both of whom made many perceptive criticisms and suggestions, enabling me to make my treatment of the subject less imperfect than it would otherwise have been. The author alone, of course, is responsible for the views expressed, and any deficiencies which remain in the book as it stands.

I am also grateful to the Research Committee of the University College of Rhodesia and Nyasaland, and to its Chairman, Dr. Walter Adams, Principal of the College, for assistance with various aspects of the publication. To Ashbel G. Brice, Director of the Duke University Press, I am grateful for commendable patience and friendly assistance. Finally, the last word is reserved for the author's wife, without whose encouragement and secretarial labors publication would not have been possible. Her assistance has been invaluable.

W. L. Taylor.

University College of Rhodesia and Nyasaland,
Salisbury,
Southern Rhodesia.
December, 1957;

and

University of Otago,
Dunedin,
New Zealand.
May, 1964.

TABLE OF CONTENTS

In the manufacture of economic wisdom, each of us should expend his little fund of energy, partly on the fixed capital of the deductive *organon* and partly on the materials of historical experience.

—F. Y. Edgeworth, "The Objects and Methods of Political Economy," republished in *Papers Relating to Political Economy* (London: Macmillan and Co., Limited, 1925), I, 11.

PART ONE

INTRODUCTION

CHAPTER I

FRANCIS HUTCHESON AND THE SCOTTISH ENLIGHTENMENT

It is chiefly in the description of Adam Smith's intellectual progress and the analysis of influences which went to make the Wealth of Nations *that there may be room for something further.*[1]

A frequently occurring misunderstanding in the history of economic thought is that most of the pre-Smithian economic literature can be divided readily into two sharply distinct categories. It is often rather naïvely held that this large body of economic discussion can be conveniently and legitimately classified into a dichotomy between "the commercial system," as the term is used by Smith, and a gradually growing body of economic liberalism. Apart from the many difficulties inherent in framing universally accepted definitions of these rather vague classifications, this kind of approach to what is after all a rich, burgeoning period in British economic literature—a period embellished with great new intellectual development—reduces to the grounds of unwarranted generalization some of the more fruitful sources of the future development of economic doctrines.

Before March 9, 1776,[2] only two authors—Richard Cantillon and a long-exiled Scotsman, Sir James Steuart—had

---

1. J. M. Keynes, "Adam Smith As Student and Professor," *Economic History,* III (Feb., 1938), 33.
2. Publication date of the *Wealth of Nations.*

published sets of consistently developed economic principles.[3] It is interesting to note, in passing, that Steuart's compatriot Adam Smith, who has been popularly but mistakenly deified as "the father of political economy," chose to ignore completely almost a decade later the many valuable contributions made to the stream of economic thought by Sir James Steuart,[4] although he makes some acknowledgment of his debt to Cantillon.

Only these two pre-Smith publications can qualify as valid attempts to formulate and propound sets of logically derived principles, aimed at clarifying the economic phenomena of society. Nevertheless, sixteenth-, seventeenth-, and eighteenth-century economic literature abounded in variegated and extensive economic inquiries of a fragmentary nature.

These centuries of economic investigation, inquiry, debate, and controversy produced a comprehensive body of economic literature. While the theoretical content of the outpouring of pamphlets and minor works does not yield easily to precise interpretation and classification, it was from this heterogeneous body of literature that Adam Smith drew much of the inspiration he needed to fashion the "box of economic tools" with which he constructed his *Wealth of Nations*. While it is not my object to examine the many and diverse elements which form the corpus of pre-Smithian

3. Richard Cantillon, *Essai sur la nature du commerce en général*, ed. Henry Higgs (London: Frank Cass and Co. Ltd., 1959). This book was probably written between 1730 and 1734, but not published until 1755. Sir James Steuart, *An Inquiry into the Principles of Political Oeconomy* (2 vols.; London: A. Millar and T. Cadell, 1767). For a sound account of Steuart's economics, S. R. Sen, *The Economics of Sir James Steuart* (London: G. Bell and Sons, Ltd., 1957) should be consulted. For an outline of Steuart's life, see W. L. Taylor, "A Short Life of Sir James Steuart: Political Economist," *The South African Journal of Economics*, XXV (Sept., 1957), 290–302.

4. In a letter to Sir William Pulteney dated September 5, 1772, Adam Smith wrote: "I have the same opinion of Sir James Stewart's book that you have. Without once mentioning it, I flatter myself that any fallacious principle in it will meet with a clear and distinct confutation in mine." Quoted from John Rae, *Life of Adam Smith* (London: Macmillan & Co., 1895), 253–254.

political economy, it is salutary, nevertheless, to state what is, perhaps, the main general characteristic of the works of these early authors. Not one of them, except the two mentioned above, attempted to build a logical, consistent, completely integrated theory of the economic principles which motivate the behavior of the society each is trying to describe. The one common feature of most of their works, if one can be discerned at all, is their fragmentary nature and thought.

Towards the end of this period, however, a small but select group of Scottish moral philosophers concerned themselves with the task of establishing an experimental basis for the study of man in relation to the customs and organization of a civilized community. These philosophers were intimately linked by warm personal ties of friendship, and, stimulated by the close relationship of teacher and pupil, they formed a vastly influential philosophical group. This study concerns itself with some of the major economic contributions of three of the chief members of the group—Francis Hutcheson, David Hume, and Adam Smith—and the degree of similarity between their respective views.

This was an outstanding period in Scottish intellectual life: it was a period of rapid change and increasing prosperity, and against this background the Scottish Enlightenment occurred.[5] One of the most influential developments was the birth of new life and enthusiasm in the Scottish universities. These all had their share of famous scholars. John Monro, responsible for Edinburgh's pre-eminence in medicine; James Hutton, the geologist; MacLauren, the interpreter of Newton; and John Playfair, the mathematician, were some of the leading figures in this upsurge in Scottish intellectual life. English universities at this time were completely overshadowed by their northern rivals, and

---

5. *Vide* Gladys Bryson, *Man and Society: The Scottish Inquiry of the Eighteenth Century* (Princeton: Princeton University Press, 1945).

existed, it seems, for the benefit of their academic staffs only.[6]

One of the men chiefly responsible for the new spirit of enlightenment in the Scottish universities was Francis Hutcheson, who was both a stimulating teacher and a liberal in his religious and political views. Although he was not, in the most accurate sense, a Scotsman, for he was born in Ireland, he was intimately connected with Scotland by descent, education, and his association with Glasgow University for sixteen years as Professor of Moral Philosophy.[7]

In 1711 Francis Hutcheson became a student at Glasgow University, and under the teaching of little-known Gershom Carmichael his attention was first directed towards ethics and natural theology.[8] Among other teachers who greatly influenced Francis Hutcheson and who also taught Hutcheson's most celebrated pupil, Adam Smith, were Robert Simson, Professor of Mathematics, later praised by Hutcheson as "the best geometer in the world," and Alexander Dunlop, the Professor of Greek.

When Francis Hutcheson was appointed to Glasgow University as Professor of Moral Philosophy in 1730, he first taught the works of Samuel von Pufendorf and the *Compend* of his predecessor, Gershom Carmichael. Subsequently, he delivered written lectures varying from year to year which were practically the same as his *System of Moral Philosophy*.[9]

6. The comment was offered in the *London Critical Review*, XXV (Dec. 1795), that the Scottish professors of this period rescued the literature and science of Britain from the contempt into which these would otherwise have fallen.

7. William Robert Scott, *Francis Hutcheson: His Life, Teaching and Position in the History of Philosophy* (Cambridge: At the University Press, 1900). The details which follow relating to Hutcheson's life and career are taken from chap. iv of this book. See also David Murray, *Memories of the Old College of Glasgow* (Glasgow: Jackson, Wylie and Co., 1927).

8. For an appreciation of Gershom Carmichael, see W. L. Taylor, "Gershom Carmichael: A Neglected Figure in British Political Economy," *The South African Journal of Economics*, XXIII (Sept. 1955), 251–255.

9. Francis Hutcheson, *A System of Moral Philosophy in Three Books. To which is prefixed some account of the Life, Writings and Character of the*

Hutcheson arrived in Glasgow from Dublin in October, 1730, bringing about twenty of his old pupils with him. His first university reform was to discipline his class "by keeping the students to rules, catalogues, exact hours, etc., wherein there is certainly a very great decay." [10] William Leechman, Hutcheson's friend, colleague, and biographer, also mentions that instead of restricting himself to oral discussion in Latin, he inaugurated the new method of lecturing in English in the five daily lectures he gave each week.

Dugald Stewart, assessing the intellectual influence of Francis Hutcheson, wrote:

> The Metaphysical Philosophy of Scotland, and, indeed, the literary taste in general, which so remarkably distinguished Scotland during the last century, may be dated from the lectures of Dr. Francis Hutcheson in the University of Glasgow. . . . it was from this period that Scotland, after a long slumber, began again to attract general notice in the republic of letters.[11]

Stewart also commented that Hutcheson's

> great and deserved fame, however, in this country, rests *now* chiefly on the traditionary history of his Academical Lectures, which appear to have contributed very powerfully to diffuse, in Scotland, that taste for analytical discussion, and that spirit of liberal inquiry, to which the

---

Author by the Reverend William Leechman (Glasgow: R. and A. Foulis, 1755). Hutcheson's method of teaching was characterized by great animation. Refusing to adopt the general custom in the university of delivering his lectures while sitting or standing in the pulpit, he preferred to walk up and down the passageway at the end of the students' benches, talking as he walked. As he warmed to his topic, so his walk quickened and his delivery became more rapid. He was referred to as "an ambulatory professor"; as one, "in fac' gentlemen, we micht ca' a Peripatetic Pheelosopher" (David Murray, *op. cit.*, p. 144). F. W. Hirst also remarked that Hutcheson's "pen was so unequal to his tongue that Stewart applies to Hutcheson what Quintilian said of Hortensius: 'He gave a pleasure to his hearers which his readers miss.'" (*Adam Smith* [London: Macmillan & Co., Ltd., 1904], pp. 5–6).

10. Scott, *op. cit.*, 62.

11. *The Collected Works of Dugald Stewart*, ed. Sir William Hamilton (Edinburgh: T. Constable & Co., 1854), I, 428.

world is indebted for some of the most valuable productions of the eighteenth century.[12]

Playing a full and prominent part in the Scottish Enlightenment of this period, then, was this closely knit group of social philosophers: Hutcheson, Hume, and Smith. Both Hume and Smith knew Hutcheson, and both were directly in his intellectual tradition.

Theories of the origin and forms of government were an aspect of the study of the institutions of society which were, at that time, almost hackneyed in the treatment they received. One aspect of political problems which was seriously studied for almost the first time was that which eventually became the study of political economy. Here, of course, the outstanding name is that of Adam Smith. He fused together, with original ideas of his own, the theories of some of his predecessors and developed a comprehensive analysis of the growth of the national economy. Behind Smith stood several authors from whom he obtained many points and ideas. The works of Pufendorf carried great weight with Smith, as they had previously with Francis Hutcheson.[13] Pufendorf's ideas had been conveyed to Adam Smith by his teacher at Glasgow, Francis Hutcheson, who, in his turn, had been taught

---

12. *Ibid.*, X, 82.

13. Samuel von Pufendorf (1632–1694), born in Saxony, studied theology and jurisprudence at Leipzig and natural law and mathematics at Jena. In 1661 he was appointed to the Chair of International Law in the University of Heidelberg, the first chair of its kind in the world. In 1672, while Professor of Jurisprudence in the University of Lund, he published his chief work, *De Jure Naturae et Gentium, Libri Octo*, which achieved an immediate and wide success and was translated into English, French, and German. The translation into English was done by the Reverend Andrew Tooke (1673–1731), Professor of Geometry in Gresham College, London, 1691. A "fifth" edition appeared at Dublin in 1716, and another also styled the "fifth" at London in 1735. In 1673 Pufendorf published an influential abstract of this work entitled *De Officio Hominis et Civis, Libri Duo*. Held in high regard, he died in Berlin in 1694. James Bonar has this to say about him: "Pufendorf's ample economic discussions of money, price, and taxation in his treatise on *Natural Law* (bk. V.), would give him a place, though a humble one, in the history of economic theories" (*Philosophy and Political Economy* [3rd ed.; London: George Allen & Unwin Ltd., 1922], 86).

by Gershom Carmichael, who had translated Pufendorf from the German into Latin.

The purpose of this study is to show how Adam Smith is indebted to these two fellow moral philosophers and fellow Scots, Hutcheson and Hume, for many of his economic ideas and concepts. These two eminent predecessors of Smith have been selected for discussion since they were both in crucial positions to exert considerable influence over his intellectual development. The former was his teacher, while the latter, perhaps the greatest of British philosophers, was his intimate friend. When Adam Smith first came to Glasgow, Hutcheson, who was just half-way through his professorship there, delivered lectures on ethics and political economy which presented in very active germ some of the doctrines on which Smith's whole economic system was afterwards built.

There is nothing strange in the fact that Francis Hutcheson, the Professor of Moral Philosophy, should cover in the course of his lectures what seems to jaded modern eyes an inordinately large and unspecialized field of study. Like most writers of his day—David Hume, Adam Ferguson, Dugald Stewart, and Adam Smith—Hutcheson surveyed a large and unspecialized area of speculation. These Scottish philosophers began with natural theology, worked on to philosophy and logic, and thence proceeded to political economy and jurisprudence.

Both Hume and Hutcheson were deeply interested in the economic questions of their time. Both have left their notions on these questions in their written works. Hutcheson's philosophical works were neither few nor unimportant. They were widely demanded and very popular in the second half of the eighteenth century. For example, Foulis' catalogue lists eight publications for 1772, and of these no less than five were editions of various works by Hutcheson. Nevertheless, Hutcheson aspired to be a stimulating teacher rather than an eminent author, and here he was highly successful. This is in direct contrast to Hume, whose books are superb illustrations of his acute mind. Neither Hutcheson nor Hume has much to say, quantitatively speaking, on economics proper, but in a qualitative sense what they say is of great importance to those historians of economic thought—and there have been many of them [14]—concerned with tracing some of the antecedents of Adam Smith's ideas.

Although many valuable attempts have been made to assess the significance of Hutcheson's and Hume's influences on Adam Smith, all too frequently in the more general histories of economic thought Hutcheson is dismissed as an inspiring teacher, as if this was his sole claim to renown; too often, Hume is passed over, with a brief mention (in economics), as the philosopher who first realized the benefits that would flow from a policy of economic liberalism. Such cut-and-dried classifications are misleading.

It might be thought that the works of Rae,[15] Scott, and Cannan (previously mentioned) had, in particular, covered completely all aspects of Adam Smith's life, intellectual indebtedness, and the manifold influences which culminated in the *Wealth of Nations*. But the record is still incomplete.[16] It is hoped that this study will contribute something

14. In particular, the reader should consult James Bonar, *Philosophy and Political Economy* (London: The Macmillan Co., 1909); Edwin Cannan, *A Review of Economic Theory* (London: P. S. King and Son) and, edited by the same author, *Lectures of Adam Smith* (Oxford: The Clarendon Press, 1896); E. A. J. Johnson, *Predecessors of Adam Smith* (New York: Prentice-Hall Inc., 1937); David Hume, *Writings on Economics*, ed. Eugene Rotwein (Edinburgh: Nelson, 1953); and, in addition to the work already cited, two others by W. R. Scott: *Adam Smith as Student and Professor* (Glasgow: Jackson, Son & Co., 1937) and *Studies Relating to Adam Smith during the Last Fifty Years*, ed. A. L. Macfie *Proceedings of the British Academy*, XXVI (London: Humphrey Milford, 1962).

15. John Rae, *Life of Adam Smith* (London: Macmillan & Co., 1895).

16. William Letwin's *The Origins of Scientific Economics* (London: Methuen and Co., Ltd., 1963), while particularly useful for an analysis of the economic contributions of Sir Josiah Child, Nicholas Barbon, John Collins, Sir William Petty, John Locke, and Sir Dudley North, inexplicably makes no reference to Hutcheson, and, more surprisingly, no mention of David Hume. Furthermore, the author's view of Edwin Cannan's editorship of the *Wealth*

more to the general understanding of some of the intellectual influences embodied in the *Wealth of Nations.*

---

of Nations as being "admiring and self-effacing" and not "ambitious" enough
and too "prudent" seems to me to dismiss much too lightly the fine scholarship of Cannan's work, which, possibly more than any other major contribution, has enabled us to assess "how firmly" Adam Smith "stood on the
shoulders of his predecessors" (*ibid.*, p. 223).

CHAPTER II

ADAM SMITH AND FRANCIS HUTCHESON

We should do well therefore to look in Adam Smith's work for important traces of the influence of Francis Hutcheson, who was Professor of Moral Philosophy, at Glasgow, from 1729 to 1746, even if Hutcheson had been but an undistinguished member of the series of professors, instead of a teacher of unusual ability and originality, to whom Adam Smith acknowledged obligations, and of whom he used warm words of praise.[17]

In 1737, when he was approximately fifteen years of age, Adam Smith, a student with a marked love of reading and a highly retentive memory, entered Glasgow College.[18] Remaining at Glasgow until the spring of 1740, when he left to take up the Snell Exhibition at Balliol College, Oxford, he found the intellectual influences and environment at Glasgow to be most stimulating. By way of contrast, Smith remained at Oxford for six years, where he was most unhappy, and where "the greater part of the public professors have, for these many years, given up altogether even the pretence of teaching." [19]

17. *Lectures of Adam Smith,* ed. Cannan, p. xxv.
18. The date of his birth is unknown. It is usually given as June 5, 1723, but this is the date of his baptism.
19. *Wealth of Nations,* ed. Edwin Cannan (London: Methuen & Co., 1930), II, 251. See also Scott, *Adam Smith as Student and Professor,* Part I, pp. 28–45, for a full account of Smith's student days.

If a student did not previously have a fair knowledge of Latin and Greek on entry to Glasgow College, the Arts Course extended over three years. Smith immediately passed the prescribed examinations in these subjects and proceeded to a major course in Logic. A few significant details are available relating to Smith's undergraduate career at Glasgow. He certainly attended Alexander Dunlop's famous class in Greek, for there is a copy of the *Encheiridion* of Epictetus in the University Library at Glasgow with Smith's boyish autograph written on the flyleaf. There is evidence, furthermore, that Hutcheson's Moral Philosophy class was specially attractive to Smith. The works of Grotius were a tradition in this class, and the College Library possessed several copies of his major writings.[20] One of these, interestingly enough, has Smith's signature inscribed on the end paper.[21] This is an important fact, for it shows that before the age of seventeen Smith had been introduced to the concept of natural law and taught to accept the supremacy of the *lex naturalis*. Of Smith's life outside the classroom, however, unfortunately very little is known.[22] Contrary to John Rae's statement "that Smith did not complete the course required for a degree"[23] at Glasgow, Smith took his M.A. with great distinction, graduating from Glasgow in 1740 before proceeding to Oxford.[24]

During these early formative years Smith received his greatest mental stimulation and encouragement. He sat at the feet of "the never-to-be-forgotten Dr. Hutcheson," whose

20. Murray, *op.cit.*, p. 508.
21. James Bonar, "Adam Smith's Library," *The Economic Journal*, XLVI (March, 1936), 180.
22. For an excellent account of the Scotland in which Smith lived and wrote, see C. R. Fay, *Adam Smith and the Scotland of His Day* (Cambridge: Cambridge University Press, 1956). See also, by the same author, *The World of Adam Smith* (Cambridge: W. Heffer and Sons, Ltd., 1960) for a fascinating account of Smith in relation to the economy of his period, as depicted in the *Wealth of Nations*.
23. *Op.cit.*, p. 9.
24. Scott, *Adam Smith as Student and Professor*, pp. 36, 137, and 392.

stimulating lectures presented him with his first exciting ideas about political economy and economic liberalism. Hutcheson exerted the most powerful and enduring influence upon the cast of Smith's mind. No other man, including his close friend David Hume, did as much to guide the development of his intellectual awakening and mould his ideas as did Francis Hutcheson, the "new light in the University."

Hutcheson was a forceful, stimulating teacher possessing the rare gift of eloquent expression, freshness of thought, and earnestness of manner which obtained for him a firm hold over the minds of his students. William Leechman, his colleague and biographer, felt that:

> Such abilities, such dispositions, and such stores of knowledge, as have been mentioned, accompanied with a happy talent, of speaking with ease, with propriety and spirit, rendered him one of the most masterly and engaging teachers that have appeared in our age.[25]

In commenting on Hutcheson's remarkable personal characteristics as a teacher, W. R. Scott writes as follows:

> The key-note will be found in the fact that he was a Professor-preacher, intertwining, in a double expression, two different gospels, one the claim for the modern spirit, for light and culture, the enthusiasm for Benevolence and Beauty; and the other, of an artistic nature, in so far as he endeavoured to mould the plastic young minds around him into so many living realisations of his ethical ideal.[26]

Scott quotes another view of Hutcheson:

> "A more powerful testimony is that written as late as 1772—thirty-six years after Hutcheson's death—expressly to discredit the methods of teaching at Glasgow. Amidst universal censure the writer is constrained to speak in high terms of "this illustrious teacher of morality, himself a

---

25. Hutcheson, *A System of Moral Philosophy in Three Books*, I, xxx–xxxi.
26. *Francis Hutcheson, His Life, Teaching and Position in the History of Philosophy*, pp. 64–65.

perfect and ready master of Greek and Latin. He introduced or revived a high taste for Classical learning in this place, and, while he lived, he kept it alive. If ever a Professor had the art of communicating knowledge; if ever one had the magical power to inspire the hearts of youth with an admiration and love of virtue; if ever one had the art to create an esteem for Liberty and a contempt for tyranny and tyrants, he was the man! What a pity it was that, for three or four months a year, such superior talents should have been thrown away on metaphysical and fruitless disputations! When these were got over, how delightful and edifying it was to hear him!" [27]

Dugald Stewart also adds his words of praise of Hutcheson as a lecturer:

The lectures of the profound and eloquent Dr. Hutcheson, which he [Smith] had attended, previous to his departure from Glasgow, and of which he always spoke in terms of the warmest admiration, had, it may be reasonably presumed, a considerable effect in directing his talents to their proper objects.[28]

And again:

. . . those who have derived their knowledge of Dr. Hutcheson from his publications may perhaps be inclined to dispute the propriety of the epithet eloquent, when applied to the *System,* which was published after his death, as the substance of his Lectures in the University of Glasgow. His talents, however, as a public speaker, must have been of a far higher order than what he has displayed as a writer; all his pupils whom I have happened to meet with (some of them certainly, very competent judges) having agreed exactly with each other in their account of the extraordinary impression which they made on the minds of his hearers. I have mentioned, in the text, Mr. Smith as one of his warmest admirers, and to his name I shall take the opportunity of adding those of the late Earl of Selkirk, the late Lord President Miller, and the late Dr.

27. *Ibid.,* pp. 75–76. Scott is quoting from *The Defects of an University Education* (London: 1772), p. 9.
28. *The Collected Works of Dugald Stewart,* X, 8.

Archibald Maclaine, the very learned and judicious translator of Mosheim's Ecclesiastical History. My father too, who had attended Dr. Hutcheson's lectures for several years, never spoke of them without much sensibility.[29]

Not only did Hutcheson possess these natural personal advantages but, as mentioned earlier, he was the first professor in Glasgow to give up lecturing in Latin, and speak in his own tongue with great freedom and animation and without notes. Such an expressive and eloquent teacher was bound to influence and inspire deeply his admiring students.

He regarded the culture of the heart as a main end of all moral instruction; he kept it habitually in view, and he was extremely well qualified for succeeding in it, so far as human means can go; he had an uncommon vivacity of thought and sensibility of temper, which rendered him quickly susceptible of the warmest emotions upon the great subjects of morals and religion; this gave a pleasant unction to his discourses which commanded the attention of the students, and at the same time, left strong impressions upon their minds.[30]

In his lectures on government, which probably gave Smith his first taste of economics, Hutcheson emphasized the then very topical question of civil and religious liberty.

As he had occasion every year in the course of his lectures to explain the origin of government, and compare the different forms of it, he took peculiar care, while on that subject, to inculcate the importance of civil and religious liberty, and manly zeal for promoting it; . . . he always insisted upon it at great length, and with the greatest strength of argument and earnestness of persuasion, and he had such success on this important point, that few, if any, of his pupils, whatever contrary prejudices they might bring along with them ever left him without favourable notions

29. *Ibid.*, p. 81.
30. Leechman's Introduction, in Hutcheson, *op.cit.*, I, xxxi–xxxii.

of that side of the question, which he espoused and defended.[31]

For three formative, impressionable years, Adam Smith was under the influence of the religious optimism and strong love of liberty which graced the teaching of Francis Hutcheson, and he was to be influenced by these ideas for the rest of his life.

Quite apart from his lecture-room activities, Hutcheson added another interesting and novel branch to his work in Glasgow College. Many complaints had been made during his period there about the inaccessibility and lack of interest shown by the professors in the students' everyday life. Hutcheson set out to remedy this position and he became, where necessary, the guardian, friend, and even banker to those students who needed his guidance and advice.[32]

That Smith regarded Hutcheson with a warm and friendly feeling is illustrated by the following extract from one of his letters. On being appointed to the position of Rector of Glasgow University in November, 1787, Smith wrote to the Reverend Dr. A. Davidson, Principal of Glasgow College:

> No man can own greater obligations to a Society, than I do to the University of Glasgow. They educated me, they sent me to Oxford, soon after my return to Scotland they elected me one of their own members, and afterwards preferred me to another office, to which the abilities and virtues of the never-to-be-forgotten Dr. Hutcheson had given a superior degree of illustration.[33]

Although Hutcheson's name is rarely found in the standard histories of economic doctrines, he lectured for many years on political economy as a branch of his course on natural jurisprudence. His remarks are only of a fragmentary

31. *Ibid.*, pp. xxxv–xxxvi.
32. Scott, *Francis Hutcheson*, pp. 68–69.
33. Rae, *op.cit.*, p. 411.

nature, scattered here and there throughout his works, but taken together, they are highly significant for the later development of the subject in Britain. They indicate that he had an acute and clear grasp of some highly important economic questions. His ideas were far superior to those of most of his contemporaries and foreshadow many of Adam Smith's fundamental tenets. Edwin Cannan in the Introduction to his edition of the *Lectures of Adam Smith* states that the discovery of these Glasgow *Lectures* proves that much, but not all, of the theory of the *Wealth of Nations* had been taught in Hutcheson's classes long before Smith became acquainted with the work of any of the Physiocrats.[34] In advancing the claim that Hutcheson's ideas were important in moulding Smith's economic thought, Cannan bases his case on the evidence contained in Hutcheson's *Introduction to Moral Philosophy*.[35] The discovery of more information subsequently about the life and work of Hutcheson adds evidence to this claim. It has been shown that Hutcheson had used the manuscript of the *System of Moral Philosophy* as material for his lectures about 1737.[36] Smith entered Glasgow College in that year and therefore it is reasonable to assume that as a student he became familiar with the economic contents of the *System* when he attended Hutcheson's stimulating lectures on Moral Philosophy.

Shortly after the publication of Cannan's edition of the Glasgow *Lectures,* W. R. Scott showed that the order of treatment in the economic sections of the Glasgow *Lectures* and in the *Wealth of Nations* repeated the order of treatment in Hutcheson's *System*, although as Scott cautiously remarked, ". . . the parallelism may be nothing more than coincidence." A few pages later, however, Scott goes much further and suggests that Adam Smith may have used

34. *Op. cit.*, p. xxiv.
35. Francis Hutcheson, *A Short Introduction to Moral Philosophy in Three Books* (Glasgow: R. and A. Foulis, 1742).
36. Scott, *Adam Smith as Student and Professor*, pp. 112 and 231.

Francis Hutcheson's *System* as the basic plan for the preparation of his own Glasgow *Lectures* of 1762–1763.[37] (See the accompanying Table 1, on next page.)

On the basis then of Smith's presumed intimate knowledge of Hutcheson's *System* gained by attendance at Hutcheson's lectures, and from a comparison of the contents of Hutcheson's *Introduction to Moral Philosophy* with Smith's *Lectures* of 1762–1763, we may fairly conclude that Smith was well acquainted with the economic notions expressed by his illustrious teacher, "the never-to-be-forgotten Dr. Hutcheson." It might be objected, however, that where Smith mentions the views on Moral Philosophy of authors before Hutcheson—those for example of Pufendorf, Grotius, and Locke—he had directly consulted the works of these men. No doubt he did. But when it is borne in mind that Smith heard these passages criticized and expounded by his respected teacher during his undergraduate days, and further, that the *System* which best enshrines these ideas was published in 1755, three years after Smith's appointment to the Chair of Moral Philosophy at Glasgow, it can be assumed that he became fully conversant with Francis Hutcheson's seminal economic ideas during his college days. Direct consultation with the earlier authors would probably have served only to convince Smith of the force and truth of Hutcheson's teachings.

In 1745 Francis Hutcheson published in Latin a small volume entitled *Philosophiae moralis institutio compendiaris libris III, ethices et iursprudentiae naturalis elements continens.* He authorized its translation and publication in 1747 as a *Short Introduction to Moral Philosophy in Three Books, Containing the Elements of Ethicks and the Law of Nature.*[38] Some idea can be obtained from this book of what

---

37. *Ibid.*, pp. 235, 240.
38. *Introduction to Moral Philosophy* (2nd ed.; Glasgow: Printed and Sold by Robert and Andrew Foulis. Printers to the University, 1753).

Hutcheson's SYSTEM		LECTURES, *1703*		WEALTH OF NATIONS	SUBJECTS
Bk. II Chap. IV		Pt. II Div. II Sections 3–5		Bk. I Chaps. 1, 2	Division of labor
Bk. II Chap. VI		„	„	Bk. I Chap. 5	„
Bk. II Chap. XII		„	„	Bk. I Chap. 4	Value
„	„	„	7	„ „	Value in use and in exchange
„	„	„	8	Bk. I Chaps. 4–5	Money, medium of exchange
„	„	„	7	Bk. I Chap. 7	Price
„	„	„	7	Bk. I Chap. 8	Wages
Bk. II Chap. XIII		„	14	Bk. I Chaps. 9–10	Theory and rate of interest
„	„	„	16	Bk. I Chap. 11	Explanation of rent
Bk. III Chap. IX		„	10–12	Bk. IV	State and foreign trade
„	„	Part III		Bk. V	Maxims of taxation

This table is adapted from W. R. Scott, *Francis Hutcheson, His Life, Teaching and Position in the History of Philosophy*, p. 235.

Adam Smith was taught in this field when he was Francis Hutcheson's pupil.

After the "Advertisement" comes the address "To the Students in Universities," which begins as follows:

> The celebrated division of philosophy among the ancients was into the rational or logical, the natural and the moral. Their moral philosophy contained these parts, ethics taken more strictly, teaching the nature of virtue and regulating the internal dispositions; and the knowledge of the law of nature. This latter contained,
>
> 1. the doctrine of *private rights*, or the laws obtaining in natural liberty.
> 2. *Oeconomicks*, or the laws and rights of several members of a family; and
> 3. *Politicks*, showing the various plans of civil government, and the rights of states with respect to each other.[39]

Accordingly, Francis Hutcheson entitled these three books:

Book I. The Elements of Ethicks.

Book II. Elements of the Laws of Nature.

Book III. The Principles of Oeconomicks and Politicks.

Adam Smith's *Theory of Moral Sentiments* [40] or to give it its full title, *An Essay towards an Analysis of the Principles by which Men naturally judge concerning the Conduct and Character, first of their Neighbours and afterwards of themselves,* closely corresponds with Francis Hutcheson's Book I of the *Introduction to Moral Philosophy,* "The Elements of Ethicks."

"Private Law," which is Division III of Adam Smith's *Lectures on Justice,* corresponds with Hutcheson's Book II of the *Introduction,* called "Elements of the Laws of Nature." The first two divisions of Adam Smith's *Lectures on Justice*—"Public Jurisprudence" and "Domestic Law"—correspond with Hutcheson's Book III of the *Introduction,* "The Principles of Oeconomicks and Politicks." Each author's

39. *Ibid.,* v.
40. Edinburgh: John D. Lowe, 1844.

treatment is characteristically his own, but the main subjects dealt with are, roughly speaking, the same. There is, however, one important difference in that neither Adam Smith's chapter in the *Lectures* on "Revenue," nor his chapter on "Arms" corresponds to anything in Hutcheson's works; nearly the same may be said of his chapter on "Police." For Hutcheson's discussion of the subjects covered by Smith in this chapter (see below, pp. 23–25)—and his most significant economic discussion, we must turn to Book II, Chapter XII of the *Introduction to Moral Philosophy*, "Concerning the Value or Prices of Goods." [41] The logical link between this economically interesting chapter and the preceding [42] and succeeding [43] chapters is disjointed. In writing it, Hutcheson appears merely to have reproduced almost unchanged many of the ideas of Pufendorf, Grotius, and Locke on political and economic questions.[44]

Both Hutcheson's *System* and his *Introduction to Moral Philosophy* are badly arranged. The first book in each case deals with ethics, the second book begins with ethical investigations and continues with rights and property, while the third book analyzes and discusses some economic ideas and the theory of the state. At first sight, it would appear that there was little conceptual similarity on economic questions between Hutcheson's *System* and Adam Smith's Glasgow *Lectures*. But this is a misleading conclusion, for in substance the difference between the two books is insignificant; the differences are mainly those of arrangement and presentation of material. Smith is quite explicit about his intention to reverse the order of arrangement and treatment followed by former authors:

41. See also Hutcheson, *A System of Moral Philosophy*, II, 53–64.
42. "Of Oaths and Vows."
43. "Of the Several Sorts of Contracts."
44. See Scott, *Francis Hutcheson, His Life, Teaching and Position in the History of Philosophy*, p. 231.

Others who have written on this subject begin with the latter, (property and other rights) and then consider family and civil government. (As Francis Hutcheson does in the Introduction to Moral Philosophy). There are several disadvantages peculiar to each of these methods, though that of the civil law seems upon the whole preferable.[45]

In his lectures at Glasgow University Smith dealt first with ethics (separately and much more fully represented by his *The Theory of Moral Sentiments,* first published in 1759). He also handled economic questions separately under the heading of "Police" in Part II, Division II of the *Lectures,* in the subsection, "Cheapness and Plenty."[46] The general treatment and ordering of material followed by teacher and pupil is shown in the accompanying table, which also illustrates how Smith reversed the order of treatment and selection of topics chosen by Hutcheson.

For some obscure, unknown reason, Hutcheson sandwiched his most crucial economic chapter, "Concerning the Values or Prices of Goods," between a chapter on "Oaths and Vows" and one on the "Several Sorts of Contracts" in his *Introduction to Moral Philosophy.* When Smith began his academic teaching career, he no doubt saw the incongruity of this apparently haphazard positioning. He decided that

45. *Lectures of Adam Smith,* ed. Cannan, p. 8.
46. *Ibid.,* pp. 157–236.
Apparently Smith also attempted to model his lecture-room procedure on Hutcheson's characteristic style, for it has been recorded that Smith "made a laudable attempt at first to follow Hutcheson's animated manner, lecturing on Ethics without papers, walking up and down his class-room, but not having the same facility in this that Hutcheson had . . . soon relinquished the attempt and read with propriety all the rest of his valuable lectures from the desk" (Murray, *op. cit.,* p. 144).
Like Hutcheson, too, in other respects, Smith took a deep interest in his students, which was most unusual for university teachers at that time. "He was at great pains to discover and cherish the seeds of genius; and, therefore, when he met with acute, studious young men he invited them to his house, that from the turn of their conversation he might discover the bents and intent of their faculties. He took great pleasure in directing their studies and solving their doubts adapting his hints to their plan of life" (*ibid.,* p. 393).

TABLE TWO

	Hutcheson's INTRODUCTION TO MORAL PHILOSOPHY *1747*	Hutcheson's SYSTEM OF MORAL PHILOSOPHY *1755*	Smith's GLASGOW LECTURES *1703*
	Book 2 Chaps. 6–9	Book 2 Chaps. 6–13	Part 1 Division 3 (Private Law)
Subject matter treated in:	Book 3 Chaps. 1–3	Book 3 Chaps. 1–3	Part 1 Division 2 (Domestic Law)
	Book 3 Chaps. 4–8	Book 3 Chaps. 4–8	Part 1 Division 1 (Public Jurisprudence)

it would be an improvement in logical arrangement to transfer the contents of this important chapter to a new heading. He called it "Police" since the regulation of prices and the creation of coinage both came under the meaning of this word as it was used at that time. As he continued to lecture and think about these subjects year by year, the concept of money and prices must have assumed larger and larger proportions in his mind, for the subject developed to embrace many topics not usually regarded as part of "Police," as the term was then understood. It must have been in some such way as this that the second and most important part of "Police," "Cheapness and Plenty," assumed the final form we know today.

Although the nature of the subject matter discussed by the two men is roughly similar, a reading of their works shows that Smith's treatment, besides reversing Hutcheson's arrangement of topics, is markedly in advance of Hutcheson's on some, but not all, matters. In many ways perhaps, it is a little unjust to assess the importance and value of Hutcheson's contributions to philosophy and political economy on the basis of his written works. For the historian of economic doctrine, however, it is the only objective criterion that may be legitimately used. In fact, Hutcheson's books are only a faint shadow of the personal attraction, magnetism, and dynamic character he displayed within the lecture room. The latter was his true *milieu,* not the written word.[47] His life's work was to mould character and personalities, and he felt that the authorship was always secondary to this primary aim. By comparison, the much more sedate and phlegmatic Smith produced books characterized by a wealth of historical detail and illustration, indicative of a superior sense of authorship in the pupil.

In the address "To The Students in Universities," previously mentioned, Hutcheson described his *Introduction to Moral Philosophy* in this way:

> The learned will at once discern how much of this compound is taken from the writings of others, from Cicero and Aristotle; and to name no other moderns, from Pufendorf's smaller work, *De Officio Hominis et Civis Juxta Legem Naturalem* which that worthy and ingenious man the late Professor Gershom Carmichael of Glasgow, by far the best commentator on that book, has so supplied and corrected that the notes are of much more value than the text.[48]

Although Pufendorf's economic sections are few, they are of considerable importance in tracing the antecedents of some of Adam Smith's economic views. Pufendorf's doctrines

---

47. For further description of Hutcheson's oratorical power and influence on students at Glasgow College, see John Veitch, "Philosophy in Scottish Universities," *Mind*, II (Jan., 1877), 207–212.
48. Hutcheson, *op. cit.*, p. v.

reached Adam Smith via the teaching of Hutcheson, who in his turn had as his teacher Gershom Carmichael, "by far the best commentator" (on Pufendorf's *De Officio*). In the history of the development of Scottish philosophical thought, Carmichael ranks as the founder of independent investigation. His appointment to the Chair of Moral Philosophy at Glasgow marks the beginning of independent Scottish inquiry.[49]

Carmichael's course of lectures at Glasgow University was divided into two parts. One portion embraced Moral Philosophy, while the other was devoted to Natural Theology. His first work, published in 1718, was his *System of Natural Theology*. In 1720 he published at Glasgow his *Breviuscula Introductio ad Logicam*, a treatise on logic.[50] His greatest achievement, however, was to translate Pufendorf's *De Officio*, to which he added notes and a supplement of considerable merit. This was first published at Glasgow in 1718 by Donald Govan, the university printer. Apparently it was carelessly printed; a second, improved edition of the text and of Carmichael's 116 pages of supplements and notes was published in 1724 and subsequently reprinted again at Leyden in 1769.[51] The importance of this work and its most notable advance is the subordination of jurisprudence to ethics, and the attempt to ground human laws in the observation and analysis of the observed characteristics of human nature. Carmichael's *Synopsis Theologiae Naturalis*, published at Edinburgh in the year of his death, 1729, shows that while he retained traces of the dying formalism

---

49. See Taylor, *op. cit.* Carmichael was the first Professor of Moral Philosophy appointed in the University of Glasgow, in 1727.

50. "Carmichael published an *Abstract of Logick* for his class, and Pufendorf's *De Officio* with notes, which took so well that it bore two editions . . . . for these twelve or fifteen years last he was of very great reputation, and was exceedingly valued both at home and abroad" (Robert Wodrow, *Analecta, or Materials for a History of Remarkable Providences Mostly Relating to Scotch Ministers and Christians,* ed. Matthew Leishman [Edinburgh: Printed for the Maitland Club, 1842–1843], IV, 96).

51. Murray, *op. cit.,* p. 509.

of his time, he gave due weight to the new and experimental method of founding inference on the observation of facts. While the beginnings of fresh thought did not develop greatly in Carmichael, they were expanded in the mind of his more famous pupil—Francis Hutcheson.

All in all, Carmichael has left a respected and notable name as a thinker. He was, in Glasgow University, the bridge between the old thought and the new, well read in the older philosophy but alive to a new power and method of inquiry.[52] Carmichael marks a period of transition from the rigid Calvinism of his own day to the flowering of metaphysical philosophy which was brought about in Scotland mainly through the zeal and enthusiasm of Francis Hutcheson.

For these reasons, then, together with the fact that he was Hutcheson's teacher, some understanding of Carmichael's life and work is necessary. By making the contents of Pufendorf's works available for general study, and by interpreting Pufendorf's valuable ideas to his students, and in particular to Francis Hutcheson, Carmichael fulfilled a most influential and important service. It is known, for example, that Hutcheson at the beginning of his teaching career in Glasgow taught Pufendorf on the basis of Carmichael's translation and commentary.

> About this time Mr. Hutcheson came to Glasgow, and about eighteen or twenty of his former students at Dublin with him. He is well spoke of. He teaches Mr. Carmichael's *Compound* and Pufendorf, and speaks with much veneration of him.[53]

The interesting point for the development of economic thought in all this is the very close parallelism between Pufendorf's *De Officio* and Hutcheson's *Introduction to*

---

52. "I hear that, on Mr. Carmichael's death, all the English Students have left the University; and, indeed, it's very thin this winter, and his name and reputation brought many to it" (*Analecta*, pp. 190–191).

53. *Ibid.*, p. 185.

Moral Philosophy. Each man covered almost exactly the same field. Indeed, Hutcheson's treatment of value is almost identical with that of Pufendorf, as is shown in a subsequent chapter. The inescapable conclusion is that Francis Hutcheson took over almost in whole, from Carmichael, the economic ideas of Pufendorf and, in the course of time, passed them on to Adam Smith.

CHAPTER III

ADAM SMITH AND DAVID HUME

> *Only within the small circle of Edinburgh*
> *intellectuals was his (Hume's) genius fully*
> *appreciated, though not fully approved, and of that*
> *intimate group only his closest friend Adam Smith*
> *gave the nod of whole-hearted approval.*[54]

Some writers, after scarcely acknowledging the merits of Francis Hutcheson's economic ideas, proceed to emphasize the nature of the intellectual debt owed by Smith to David Hume. There is, however, a great deal in common in the general field of economic inquiry and analysis in the work of Hutcheson and Hume. While it cannot be stated for certain how and when they first came into contact with each other, enough is known about their relationship to conclude that not only were they close personal friends, but that Hume showed great respect for Hutcheson's philosophical ideas.

In September, 1739, in his first recorded letter to Hutcheson, Hume wrote, in part, as follows:

> I am much obliged to you for your reflections on my papers. I have perused them with care, and find they will be of use to me. You have mistaken my meaning in some passages; which upon examination I have found to proceed from some ambiguity or defect in my expressions. . . . I have many other reflections to communicate to you; but it would

54. Mossner, *op. cit.*, p. 4.

be troublesome. I shall therefore conclude with telling you, that I intend to follow your advice in altering most of those passages you have remarked as defective in point of prudence; though I must own, I think you are a little too delicate. . . . I hope you will allow me the freedom of consulting you when I am in any difficulty; and believe me to be,

    Dear Sir,

          Your most obliged humble servant,

              David Hume.[55]

Ninewells near
Berwick,
    Sept. 17, 1739.

The papers mentioned in this letter form the manuscript of the as yet unpublished Book III "Of Morals" of Hume's *Treatise*. This letter, together with several others in Greig's edition of Hume's *Letters*, indicate that David Hume regarded Francis Hutcheson as a valuable friend and as a master of philosophy. Hume deeply valued and eagerly sought Hutcheson's advice and discussion of philosophical questions.[56]

The next letter to pass between the two correspondents is a most significant one, since it has been the source of a frequently recurring error in the history of the relationship between the two men. The relevant extracts from the letter follow:

Dear Sir,
    Since I saw you, I have been very busy in correcting and finishing that Discourse concerning Morals, which you perus'd; and I flatter myself, that the alterations which I have made have improv'd it very much both in point of Prudence and Philosophy. I shall set out for London in three Weeks or a Month with an Intention of publishing it. The Bookseller, who printed the first two Volumes, is very

55. *The Letters of David Hume*, ed. J. Y. T. Greig (Oxford: The Clarendon Press, 1932) I, 32.

56. For a discussion of this point, see Norman Kemp Smith, *The Philosophy of David Hume* (London: Macmillan and Co., 1949), pp. 23–51.

willing to engage for this, and he tells me that the sale of the first Volumes, tho' not very quick, yet it improves. . . .
My Bookseller has sent to Mr. Smith a Copy of my Book, which I hope he has receiv'd, as well as your Letter. I have not yet heard what he has done with the Abstract. Perhaps you have. I have got it printed in London, but not in the *Works of the Learned*; there having been an article with regard to my Book, somewhat abusive, printed in that work, before I sent up the Abstract.
Your most obedient and most
humble servant,
David Hume.
Ninewells near Berwick.
March 4, 1740.
Mr. Hutcheson   Professor of Philosophy   at Glasgow.[57]

It has been wrongly conjectured by several commentators that this letter, written in 1740, records the first contact between Adam Smith and David Hume. It was apparently Hutcheson's practice to ask his students to make abstracts of newly published philosophical works as they appeared. In view of this custom it was assumed for some time that Adam Smith, although only a youth of about seventeen at the time, prepared the *Abstract* mentioned in Hume's letter.[58] It was further assumed that Smith's *Abstract* had been so excellently prepared that Hutcheson, very pleased with Smith's work, had sent it to Hume, who, in turn, had the *Abstract* printed in London and sent Smith a complimentary copy of the published work. It is of interest to note how this belief has been accepted, especially by the biographers of David Hume and Adam Smith.

It was J. H. Burton's view that the "Smith" referred to, "notwithstanding the universality of the name, was Adam Smith" and that the letter marked:

the first introduction to each other's notice, of two friends, of whom it can be said, that there was no third person

57. *The Letters of David Hume*, I, 37–38.
58. Of Hume's *Treatise of Human Nature*, Books I and II.

writing the English language during the same period, who had so much influence upon the opinions of mankind as either of these two men.[59]

Burton, however, did not connect Adam Smith with the authorship of the *Abstract*.

John Rae, Smith's distinguished biographer, carried the story a step further. He tentatively suggested that Adam Smith, under Francis Hutcheson's instructions, had written the abstract of Hume's *Treatise*, which so pleased Hume that he gave Smith a copy of the published *Abstract*.[60]

W. R. Scott, writing a short time after Rae's book appeared, reinforced the conclusions of Burton and Rae when he commented:

> Both Burton and Mr. Rae, the biographer of Adam Smith, agree in thinking that this refers to the future economist. . . . From Carlyle's *Autobiography* we learn that it was customary for Hutcheson and Leechman to require promising members of their classes to prepare abstracts either of new or standard works. . . . In this case, Hutcheson evidently sent the abstract to Hume, who thought it worthy of being printed.[61]

In a later book, however, Scott, convinced by new evidence, corrected the error of fact that he made in 1900.[62]

Conclusive evidence about the identity of the "Mr. Smith" referred to has been produced in the Introduction to a reprint of Hume's *Abstract of a Treatise on Human Nature* prepared by J. M. Keynes and P. Sraffa.[63] They make out a convincing case to prove that the mysterious "Mr. Smith" is

---

59. *Life and Correspondence of David Hume* (Edinburgh: William Tait: 1846), I, 117.
60. *Life of Adam Smith* (London: Macmillan and Co., 1895), pp. 15–16.
61. *Francis Hutcheson, His Life, Teaching and Position in the History of Philosophy*, pp. 120–121.
62. W. R. Scott, *Adam Smith As Student and Professor* (Glasgow: Jackson, Son and Company, 1937), pp. 34–35.
63. *An Abstract of a Treatise of Human Nature, 1740: A Pamphlet hitherto unknown by David Hume*, reprinted with an Introduction by J. M. Keynes and P. Sraffa (Cambridge: The University Press, 1938).

not Adam Smith the economist, but Francis Hutcheson's Dublin publisher, Mr. John Smith. It appears that the *Abstract* in question was written by David Hume himself, and published under the title of *An Abstract of a Book lately Published: Entitled, A Treatise of Human Nature, etc. Wherein the Chief Argument of that Book is further Illustrated and Explained.* Keynes and Sraffa were unaware of this title; only three copies of the original are extant.[64]

While this instance shows how details of the life of Adam Smith consist of traps for the unwary, the letter also illustrates (together with two others)[65] how Hume greatly valued the expert criticism by Hutcheson of Hume's philosophical work and the close friendship between them.

Indeed, the nature of the close relationship existing between Hume and Hutcheson suggests that even if the third member of the trio, Adam Smith, had not been Hutcheson's pupil and heard his philosophical lectures—lectures which had a far more abiding influence than his publications—many of Hutcheson's views on economic questions would probably have found their way into Smith's thinking by way of the warm friendship and close intellectual relationship that existed between Smith and Hume. Dugald Stewart has this to say on the matter: "The Political Discourses of Mr. Hume were evidently of greater use to Mr. Smith, than any other book that had appeared prior to his Lectures."[66]

From about 1752 onwards, a deep and abiding friendship grew up between Smith and Hume. Although Smith was, at best, an indolent correspondent, due partly to the difficulty he suffered from throughout his life in the physical act of writing, which was always painful and laborious to

---

64. For further details of this rather curious story, see E. C. Mossner, *The Life of David Hume* (Edinburgh: Thomas Nelson and Sons Ltd., 1954), pp. 120–124.
65. *Letters of David Hume*, I, 38–40 and 45–48.
66. Stewart, *op. cit.*, X, 66.

him, enough evidence as to the growth of their friendship is to be found in their correspondence with each other.

The first letter recorded by Greig from Hume to Smith is dated September 24, 1752.[67] It is not, as would be expected, markedly intimate in tone, but it initiated their relationship, and during the next decade the letters between the two men became much warmer and more cordial—the product of their growing association. In 1759 David Hume wrote to Adam Smith as follows:

> I give you thanks for the agreeable present of your *Theory.* [*Theory of Moral Sentiments*, Smith's first book just published by Millar.] Wedderburn and I made presents of our copies to such of our acquaintances, as we thought good judges, and proper to spread the reputation of the book.[68]

Between 1759 and 1763 a rather desultory but friendly series of letters was exchanged. A few extracts from David Hume's letters will suffice to illustrate the kind of intimacy that had grown between these two leaders of Scottish intellectual life.

> I am as lazy a correspondent as you; yet my anxiety about you makes me write.
>
> By all accounts, your book, *Wealth of Nations*, has been printed long ago; yet it has never been so much as advertised. What is the reason? If you wait till the fate of America be decided you must wait long.
>
> By all accounts, you intend to settle with us this spring; yet we hear no more of it: What is the reason? Your chamber in my house is always unoccupied: I am always at home; I expect you to land here.[69]

When at last, Adam Smith published the *Wealth of Nations* on March 9, 1776, the enthusiastic Hume thus congratulated the author:

67. *Letters of David Hume*, I, 167.
68. *Ibid.*, p. 303.
69. *Ibid.*, II, 308.

Euge! Belle! Dear Mr. Smith,

I am much pleased with your performance; and the perusal of it has taken me from a state of great anxiety. . . . it has depth, and solidity and acuteness, and is so much illustrated by curious facts that it must at least take the public attention. . . . I cannot think, that the rent of farms make any part of the price of produce, but that the price is determined altogether by the quantity and the demand. [A remarkable anticipation of Ricardo. cf. *Wealth of Nations* Book I, Chapter VI.] But these and a hundred other points are fit only to be discussed in conversation.[70]

The complete run of correspondence extant shows that for over twenty years a rich and warm friendship blossomed between these two magnificent examples of eighteenth-century Scottish intellectual inquiry. Each maintained a warm interest in the written works of the other, freely criticizing the other's works in a spirit of friendship and admiration.

David Hume, born in 1711, a decade before Adam Smith, naturally developed his philosophical and economic ideas earlier than Smith. These two intellectual giants mutually influenced each other's thinking, and it is now impossible to distinguish, in detail, the various strands of each man's contributions to the other's whole body of thought. In his role as Smith's teacher, however, Francis Hutcheson had a considerable advantage over Hume in moulding and directing Smith's receptive mind. Hutcheson probably initiated the major lines of inquiry in Smith's thinking which subsequent more intimate contact with "le bon David" served to enrich and consolidate. In the following chapters an attempt has been made to show where David Hume's ideas were taken over by Adam Smith, either in whole or in part, refurbished, and given new life within the more systematic framework enunciated by Smith.

70. *Ibid.*, pp. 311-312.

While Hume had not completely emancipated himself from some antiliberal economic notions, he showed unusual perspicuity in the few essays he devoted to economic matters. He was not deluded by the narrow prejudices of the "Mercantile System." In spite of a few errors which will be mentioned later his acute remarks on economic matters appearing in his most successful book—his *Political Discourses* (described in his autobigraphy as "the only work of mine that was successful on the first publication, well received abroad and at home") [71]—did much to dissipate some of the generally accepted antiliberal economic prejudices of the time. His acute logical sensibility, perfect clearness, and admirable precision enabled him to see and explain that the principle of domestic commerce which necessitated "an intercourse of good affairs" between the different classes of society and the different areas which were fitted by nature to supply each other's wants was just as applicable to nations as to different areas within one nation. He criticized the prevailing economic policy of emphasizing that the accumulation of money was a desirable end as being as chimerical as "the attempt to heap up water above its proper level." In fact, the *Political Discourses* contain one of the first clear refutations of the many errors inherent in the so-called "mercantile" theory. These thirteen octavo pages embody clear reasoning, extensive learning, elegant and precise language, and above all, the great merit of originality in the unfolding of new economic ideas. It is also worth noting that Hume had started to publish his *Essays, Moral and Political,* in 1741,[72] while Smith was taking up his Snell Exhibition at Oxford, although the second part of these essays, it may be supposed, with their lucid and trenchant criticism of current domestic and foreign

71. *Essays Moral, Political and Literary,* ed. T. H. Green and T. M. Grose (London: Longmans, Green and Co., 1875), I, 4.
72. Stewart, *op. cit.,* X, 66.

trade practices and policies, and highlighting the economic
significance of the difference between wealth and money,
must have confirmed Smith of the soundness of his own
early conclusions in this regard. Although Hume's discussion
of these matters is generally more original than Smith's, he
was less consistent as an enunciator of the new doctrines.
The more systematic criticism was adduced by Smith, who
had, however, much of the way paved for him by Hume's
series of brilliant, but less well-organized discussions. Certainly, Hume's essays confirmed Smith's belief in the new
principles. Professor Harold Laski describes the *Political
Discourses* as being "the most powerful dissolvent the
century was to see;"[73] Turgot thought so highly of them
that he translated several of them into French.[74]

At any rate, as early as 1749, three years before he published his *Political Discourses* and during the same year in
which Smith was advocating in Edinburgh for the first time,
his own economic ideas, David Hume clearly favored a
systems of natural liberty. In reply to a long letter from
James Oswald of Dunnikier, in which Oswald trenchantly
criticized the manuscript of Hume's essay *On the Balance of
Trade*, published in 1752 as one of the *Political Discourses*,
Hume wrote as follows:

> I never meant to say that money, in all countries which
> communicate must necessarily be on a level proportioned
> to their people, industry and commodities. That is, where
> there is double people, etc., there will be double money,
> and so on; and that the only way of keeping or increasing
> money is, by keeping and increasing the people and in-
> dustry; not by prohibitions of exporting money, or by taxes
> on commodities, the methods commonly thought of. . . .
> On the whole, my intention in the *Essay* was both to re-
> move people's errors, who are apt, from chimerical calcu-
> lations, to imagine they are losing their specie, though

73. *Political Thought in England from Locke to Bentham* (London: Oxford University Press, 1920), p. 96.
74. Stewart, *op. cit.*, X, 66–67.

they can show in no instance that either their people or their industry diminish; and also to expose the absurdity of guarding money otherwise than by watching over the people and their industry, and preserving or increasing them. To prohibit the exportation of money, or the importation of commodities is mistaken policy; and I have the pleasure of seeing you agree with me.

I have no more to say but compliments; and therefore shall conclude.

I am Dear Sir Yours Sincerely,
David Hume.

Ninewells,
1st Novr., 1750.[75]

This letter confirms the fact that as early as 1749 Hume was strongly convinced of the efficacy of a system of free trade. Thus, in view of the close similarity between Hume and Smith in this respect, it is necessary to examine Hume's work for an anticipation of many of Adam Smith's economic propositions, since Hume's economics are vitally important for the scattered but acute suggestions they contain, which later writers, particularly Adam Smith, frequently adopted.

There is no record, as far as can be established, to show that Adam Smith and David Hume had met each other before 1752 at the earliest. By this date Hume was forty years of age and Smith approaching his thirtieth birthday. Of course, they were very much aware of each other's work long before 1752. In that year Adam Smith became Professor of Moral Philosophy at Glasgow University, and, while at Glasgow, he became a founding member of the

---

75. *Letters of David Hume*, I, 142–143.
James Oswald (1715–1769) came from the same town of Kirkcaldy as Adam Smith. "The friendship of James Oswald, was, after the affection of his mother, the best thing Smith carried into life with him from Kirkcaldy" (Rae, *op. cit.*, p. 7). Oswald served as a Member of Parliament from 1741 to 1768; his administrative ability and effective public speaking won several important posts in Government for him during this period. But for his premature death at the age of fifty-four, he might have become Chancellor of the Exchequer. Both Adam Smith and David Hume held Oswald's enlightened economic opinions in high regard and they often sought out his views on their respective economic ideas.

Literary Society of that town. The society was a general debating body composed mainly of university professors and other leading Glasgow notables like Robert Foulis the printer, James Watt the inventor, and David Hume. It met every Thursday evening from November to May at 6:30 P.M. Its minutes show that at one of its first sessions, on January 23, 1753, Adam Smith read an account of some of David Hume's recently printed *Political Discourses*.[76] It is most probable that Smith had read the various essays before they were published. The following extract of a letter from Hume to Smith in September, 1752 (mentioned earlier), the first recorded letter between the two men, states:

> I am just now diverted for a moment by correcting my "Essays, Moral and Political," for a new edition. If anything occurs to you to be inserted or retrenched, I shall be obliged to you for the hint. In case you should not have the last edition by you, I shall send you a copy of it.[77]

Clearly, the two men were in close contact by this date.

Furthermore, it seems reasonably certain that Hume and Smith had met each other before the foundation of the Glasgow Literary Society, although no proof can be attested. Transcending this purely chronological question, however, and of vital importance for establishing some notion of the nature of Hume's influence on the development of Smith's economic thinking is the fact that they were in close, written contact during 1752, and possibly as early as 1750.

When Smith returned to Edinburgh in 1746, after an absence of six years at Oxford as a Snell Exhibitioner, he was unemployed for a period of two years. Reluctant to take orders in the Church of England, which was expected of Snell Exhibitioners, he was forced to find other suitable employment. In 1748 a cousin of David Hume's, Henry

---

76. Reprinted in *Essays Moral, Political and Literary*, I, 285–493.
77. *Letters of David Hume*, I, 168.

Home of Kames, later Lord Home of Kames, eager that Scottish lawyers, in particular, should enjoy a wider general education than that open to them, in association with James Oswald of Dunnikier and Robert Craigie outlined a scheme for promoting a series of public lectures in Edinburgh. Kames, a Scottish judge, was a pioneer of the rebirth of literature in Scotland and the patron of several rising young authors and philosophers, but his far-reaching influence in Edinburgh legal circles was not so much due to his literary work and endeavors, but rather to his great ability to stimulate others. In the event, this self-constituted committee of three selected as their public lecturer the newly returned Snell Exhibitioner from Balliol College, Oxford. John Rae suggests that Smith delivered these lectures at Edinburgh University.[78] A scrutiny of the Senatus, however, discloses no traces of Smith's being appointed by the university to lecture, or of a room being granted either to him or to any society for such commendable purposes.[79] It is therefore most unlikely that Edinburgh University authorized or subsidized these lectures in any way.

This was a period when public lectures were a popular form of eighteenth-century Scottish adult education. The town newspapers of that time carried many advertisements of both public and university lecture courses. Strangely enough, for what was essentially a course in adult education, there is no evidence to be found in the press that Smith's lectures received any publicity. Accordingly, it must be concluded that Kames's initiative in organizing the course of lectures was on behalf of an already existing organization. This is a feasible explanation, for Edinburgh at this time was filled with literary clubs. W. Forbes Gray, who has made a special study of Edinburgh clubs of this period, thinks that the most probable one to

78. Op. cit., pp. 31–32.
79. Scott, Adam Smith as Student and Professor, p. 48.

have authorized Smith's lectures was the Philosophical
Society of Edinburgh.[80]

Be that as it may, the question of the subject matter of
these lectures is much more important from the point of
view of tracing the originality of Smith's most famous economic propositions. It has been assumed that the three
courses dealt with modern literature and literary criticism,
except the last course. Tytler's language on this point is
inconclusive: "Adam Smith read a course of Lectures on
Rhetoric and *Belles Lettres*. He delivered these lectures at
Edinburgh in 1748 and the two following years, to a re-
spectable auditory, chiefly composed of students in law and
theology." [81] This quotation does not necessarily mean that
the complete set of lectures was wholly devoted to this one
subject. An intimate friend of Adam Smith, John Callander
of Craigforth, describes another course on civil law which
was given by Smith to those interested in jurisprudence.[82]
From the available evidence it seems that the subject matter
of Smith's Edinburgh public lectures included two courses
on literature, followed by a course on jurisprudence.[83] Unfortunately, as Rae relates, some of these lectures, together
with sixteen other volumes of manuscripts, were burnt by
Black and Hutton at Smith's request six days before his
death.[84]

Some evidence about the probable contents of this final
important course of lectures is to be found in a few sentences
written by Adam Smith in 1755.

> Man is generally considered by statesmen and projectors
> as the materials of a sort of political mechanics. Pro-

80. *Ibid.*, p. 49.
81. A. F. Tytler, *Henry Home of Kames* (Edinburgh, 1807), I, 190.
82. Scott, *op. cit.*, p. 50.
83. See Adam Smith, *Lectures on Rhetoric and Belles Lettres*, ed. J. M.
Lothian (Edinburgh: Thomas Nelson and Sons, 1963).
84. Rae, *op. cit.*, pp. 32, and 434. The Lothian edition of the *Lectures on
Rhetoric and Belles Lettres*, gives a student's notes on these lectures as they
were delivered in 1762–1763.

jector disturb nature in the course of her operations in human affairs; and it requires no more than to let her alone and give her fair play in the pursuit of her ends that she may establish her own designs. . . . Little else is requisite to carry a state to the highest degree of opulence from the lowest barbarism, but peace, easy taxes and a tolerable administration of justice; all the rest being brought about by the natural course of things. All governments which thwart this natural course, which force things into another channel or which endeavour to arrest the progress of society at a particular point are unnatural, and to support themselves are obliged to be oppressive and tyrannical.[85]

We assume that in this course Smith put forward with equally commendable firmness the doctrine of commercial freedom and industrial liberty, a doctrine absorbed originally from Francis Hutcheson.

Smith, then, no doubt developed these crucially important economic ideas as early as 1749 in his Edinburgh lectures on jurisprudence. The above quotation, at any rate, is particularly valuable for showing the relatively early development of his ideas on economic freedom. The quotation comes from a paper drawn up by Smith in 1755, the year Hutcheson's *System* was published. The paper was delivered by Smith to a society of which he was a member; he was anxious at this time to establish the originality of his ideas on certain important political and literary principles, since he was apparently apprehensive that his claims to originality would be contested by some other person or persons. Dugald Stewart had the manuscript in his possession; it contains in highly condensed form many of the more important ideas which later appeared in more systematic shape in the *Wealth of Nations*. Another extract from this paper serves to date the original appearance of these ideas:

A great part of the opinions, enumerated in this paper, is treated of at length in some lectures which I have still

85. Stewart, *op. cit.*, X, 68.

by me, and which were written in the hand of a clerk who left my service six years ago [i.e. in 1749]. They have all of them been the constant subjects of my lectures since I first taught Mr. Craigie's class, the first winter I spent in Glasgow down to this day, without any considerable variation. They had all of them been the subjects of lectures which I read at Edinburgh the winter before I left it, and I can adduce enumerable witnesses, both from that place and from this, who will ascertain them sufficiently to be mine.[86]

The antecedents, however, of Smith's main discovery, laissez-faire, are intricate and involved. In Grotius and Pufendorf the concept of natural law was made the basis of the whole legal framework. Just as Adam Smith was writing his economic lectures at Edinburgh in 1748–1749, Montesquieu published *Esprit de Lois*, in which he confined the term natural law to those functions which are permanent, mainly in man. Earlier Gershom Carmichael, the important Scottish interpreter of Pufendorf, and Hutcheson's teacher, had developed Pufendorf's ideas on the subject by extending the whole conception of natural law.[87] Francis Hutcheson, Carmichael's pupil, developed the concept still further:

'Tis plain each one has a natural right to exert his powers, according to his own judgement and inclination, for these purposes, in all such industry, labour or amusements, as are not hurtful to others in their persons or goods, while no more public interests necessarily requires his labours, or requires that his actions should be under the direction of others. This right we call *natural liberty*. Every man has a sense of this right . . . and a sense of the evil of cruelty in interrupting this joyful liberty of others, without necessity for some more general good.[88]

The first part of this quotation comes very near to being an outline of Smith's central thesis of laissez-faire. The

86. *Ibid.*
87. Scott, *op. cit.*, pp. 112–114.
88. *System of Moral Philosophy*, I, 294.

difference between Smith and Hutcheson hinges on the emphasis given to the qualifications of the main idea. The degree of difference between the two men can be seen from the following extract.

> It is the one great design of civil laws to strengthen by political sanctions the several laws of nature; and to appoint such forms of business, and of process in courts, as may prevent frauds and promote justice. The populace, often needs also to be taught, and engaged by laws, into the best methods of managing their own affairs and exercising their mechanic arts; and in general, civil laws more precisely determine many points in which the law of Nature leaves much latitude.[89]

Adam Smith, on the other hand, was more consistent and emphatic, and less tentative, in his interpretation of natural liberty. For Smith, natural law prescribed natural liberty, and from the viewpoint of principle, there was nothing else to be said on the matter.

This difference of opinion between Hutcheson's and Smith's interpretations of the scope of natural liberty, which centers on Smith's wider view of natural liberty, did not in itself provide grounds for the certain foundation of an economic system based on this concept. So far, Smith's fundamental principle was mainly deductive. But in the Edinburgh lectures (as shown in Stewart's quotation above from the 1755 lecture), Smith added the inductive confirmation of his main idea of laissez-faire, based on evidence drawn from historical data. In this way Smith attempted to demonstrate that the general result of state control of industry and commerce was usually to slow down and hinder the rate of national and individual economic progress and growth.

When Adam Smith moved to Glasgow he brought with him a great deal of material which he had previously de-

---

89. *A Short Introduction to Moral Philosophy*, p. 311.

livered at his public lectures in Edinburgh.[90] Imbedded in his lectures on jurisprudence was an important amount of data relating to economic questions, most of which reappeared, but with valuable additions, in the *Wealth of Nations*. Although the fragments of the Edinburgh lectures which Scott has discovered do not contain a clear statement of his central thesis of laissez-faire, there is no reason to doubt Smith's own words on the subject in the quotation already given from Dugald Stewart. The initial discovery had already been made and written down before he moved to Glasgow; residence there probably only confirmed and completed his belief in it.

Smith succeeded, though, in convincing the canny Glasgow merchants of the importance of his economic principles, for, as Stewart comments:

> His long residence in one of the most enlightened mercantile towns in this island, and the habits of intimacy in which he lived with the most respectable of its inhabitants, afforded him the opportunity of deriving what commercial information he stood in need of from the best sources; . . . notwithstanding the reluctance so common among men of business to listen to the conclusions of mere speculation, and the direct opposition of his leading principles to all the old maxims of trade, he was able, before he quitted his situation in the University to rank some very eminent merchants in the number of his proselytes.[91]

90. Lothian, *op. cit.*, pp. xii–xiii. Describing the reception which Smith's lectures had at Glasgow University Wodrow states: "The lectures, which were the first form of the *Theory of Moral Sentiments*, did not please Hutcheson's scholars so well as that to which they had been accustomed. The rest of his lectures were admired by them all, especially those on money and commerce" (University Library Glasgow, Murray MSS, Buchan Papers, II, 169).

91. Stewart, *op. cit.*, X, 42.
Furthermore, Murray, in discussing Smith's intimacy with the shrewd merchants of Glasgow, writes that Smith obtained from them "much information regarding commercial affairs, and it was in discussion with them, often no doubt around his own table, that many of the principles enunciated in the *Wealth of Nations* were established" (*op. cit.*, p. 393).

These Edinburgh lectures deal with commerce in a very full manner. It is possible to trace the essential ideas and rough outline of Book III of the *Wealth of Nations* and the *Glasgow Lectures* to these public lectures at Edinburgh, delivered in 1749. Fragments of these lectures, only lately discovered, substantiate this conclusion.[92] The lectures contained the groundwork of the major part of Smith's later economic work. This period is of the greatest importance for the origin of political economy, since it was then that the core of Smith's whole framework was first expounded, for by 1749 he had begun to apply the idea of natural liberty to all branches of economic activity.

These public lectures of Smith's at Edinburgh brought fame and financial success to him.[93] Some of those who attended his lectures on jurisprudence, men famous later in Scottish public life, were Wedderburn, Lord Chancellor of England in 1793; William Johnstone, later Sir William Pulteney; James Oswald of Dunnikier—his boyhood friend from Kirkcaldy who probably contributed almost as much as David Hume to the formation of Smith's early economic views; and John Callendar, a famous Scottish advocate.

Although there is no evidence to show that Smith and Hume met before 1752, it is likely that Hume attended some of the Edinburgh lectures and so established contact with Smith. Hume had been abroad part of the time (1748–1751), but returned to Edinburgh from Europe towards the end of 1748. He lived at his family home at Ninewells, near Berwick, and often visited during the winters of 1749–1750, and 1750–1751. Hume may well have attended Smith's Edinburgh lectures, particularly if they were delivered, as is surmised, before the Philosophical Society, of which Hume was a member.[94]

92. Scott, *op. cit.*, pp. 317–356, 379–385.
93. *Letters of David Hume*, I, 280.
94. "In Edinburgh, to which he [Smith] removed in 1748, literature had begun to revive; and during his residence there, a club was instituted, under

At any rate, whenever the actual date of this meeting, it was the foundation of a life-long friendship. W. R. Scott remarks: "It must have been during one of his [David Hume's] visits to Edinburgh, before Adam Smith moved to Glasgow in September or October, 1751, that the two men met." [95] This statement confirms Dugald Stewart's view of the matter:

> At what particular period his [Smith's] acquaintance with Mr. David Hume commenced, does not appear from any information that I have received; but from some papers, now in the possession of Mr. Hume's nephew, and which he has been so obliging as to allow me to peruse, their acquaintance seems to have grown into friendship before the year 1752. It was friendship on both sides founded on the admiration of genius, and the love of simplicity; and, which forms an interesting circumstance in the history of each of these eminent men, from the ambition which both have shown to record it to posterity.[96]

The conclusion that Hume and Smith had become acquainted during the period of Smith's lectures at Edinburgh is strengthened by the contents of a letter from Hume to Smith of June 8, 1758, in which Hume reminds Smith how well his lectures had been attended in Edinburgh:

---

the name of *The Select Society*. . . . In a few years it could boast, among its number, the most eminent for rank and abilities in Scotland. Of this society Mr. Smith was elected a member; but, from that diffidence which sometimes prevents men of superior talents from delivering their opinions in a mixed assembly, or it might be from some reason he did not choose to avow, it is said that he never spoke. His friend Mr. Hume was in the same predicament, and thus the debates of the society were unfortunately deprived of the support of two men, who were unquestionably inferior to none of its members. Dr. Carlyle, one of the most eminent members of the Church of Scotland, remarks this in a letter to Mr. Stewart. 'Among the most distinguished speakers in the Select Society were Sir Gilbert Elliot, Mr. Wedderburn, Mr. Andrew Pringle, Lord Kames, Mr. Walter Stewart, Lord Elibank, and Dr. Robertson. The Honourable Charles Townshend spoke once. David Hume and Adam Smith never opened their lips' " (quoted from an anonymous life of Adam Smith appearing in *The Theory of Moral Sentiments* [London: 1822], I, iii–iv).

95. Scott, *op. cit.*, p. 64.
96. Stewart, *op. cit.*, X, 10.

Pray then consider, that this is perhaps the only opportunity we shall ever have of getting you to town: I dare
swear, that you think the difference of place is worth
paying something for, and yet it will really cost you
nothing. You made above 100 pounds a year by your
class when in this place, though you had not the character
of Professor: we cannot suppose that it will be less than
130 after you are settled.[97]

The letters from Hume to Smith referred to previously
illustrate the friendship between the two men. The following additional extracts confirm the position. In a letter
written on May 3, 1776, Hume asked Smith to publish
Hume's *Dialogues Concerning Natural Religion,* a responsi-
bility that Smith could not accept. In the same letter Hume
pleaded with Smith to write to him.

I send you enclosed an ostensible letter conformably to
your desire. I think, however, your scruples groundless.
. . . I own, that your scruples have a specious appearance.
But my opinion is, that, if, upon my death you determine
never to publish these papers, you should leave them,
sealed up with my brother and family, with some inscrip-
tion, that you reserve to yourself the power of reclaiming
them, whenever you think proper. . . . By the little company I have seen, I find the town very full of your book,
[the *Wealth of Nations*] meets with general approbation.
Many people think particular points disputable; but this
you certainly expected: I am glad, that I am one of the
number, as these little points will be the subject of a
future conversation between us. . . . If you write to me,
hem! hem! I say, if you write to me, send your letters
under cover to Mr. Strahan, who will have my direction.
. . . I regret much, in leaving Edinburgh, that I shall lose
so much of your company, which I should have enjoyed
this summer.[98]

Later in that same year (November, 1776), after Hume's
death (August 25, 1776), in a letter to William Strahan,

97. *Letters of David Hume,* I, 279–280.
98. *Ibid.,* II, 316–317.

Hume's London publisher, Smith described his dear friend's character in this way:

> Thus dies our most excellent, and never-to-be-forgotten friend; concerning whose philosophical opinions man will no doubt judge variously, . . . but concerning whose character and conduct there can scarce be a difference of opinion. His temper, indeed, seemed to be more happily balanced, if I may be allowed such an expression, than that perhaps of any other man I have ever known. Even in the lowest state of his fortune his great and necessary frugality never hindered him from exercising, upon proper occasions, acts both of charity and generosity. . . . Upon the whole I have always considered him, both in his lifetime, and since his death, as approaching as nearly to the idea of a perfectly wise and virtuous man, as perhaps the nature of human frailty will admit.[99]

Less than one month after the publication of the *Wealth of Nations* Hume expressed his opinion of his friend's book in a letter to Strahan as follows: "Dr Smith's performance is another excellent work that has come from your press this winter; but I have ventured to tell him, that it requires too much thought to be as popular as Mr. Gibbon's." [100] James Boswell, writing in his diary after a deathbed interview with Hume, writes as follows: "Two particulars I remember; Smith's *Wealth of Nations* which he commended much, and Monboddo's *Origin of Language* which he treated contemptuously." [101]

Hume's last series of letters with Smith was an exchange which was delayed by Smith's "strange blunder" in sending his letter by the carrier instead of by the post. Only ten days before Hume's death he sent the following inquiry to Smith:

> Will you permit me to leave you the property of the copy [*Dialogues*] in case they should not be published in five

99. *Ibid.*, p. 452.
100. *Ibid.*, p. 314.
101. *Private Papers of James Boswell*, ed. F. A. Pottle (London: William Heineman Ltd., 1750), p. 231.

years after my decease? Be so good as to write me an answer soon. My state of health does not permit me to wait months for it.[102]

Smith did not reply until August 22. Replying on August 23, Hume wrote:

> I am obliged to make use of my nephew's hand in writing to you as I do not rise today. . . . I go very fast to decline, and last night had a small fever, which I hoped might put a quicker period to this tedious illness, but unluckily it has in a great measure gone of
> Adieu My dearest friend
> David Hume.[103]

Two days later David Hume died.

A further interesting friendship that Smith originally formed in Kirkcaldy, but strengthened in his Edinburgh days was with his fellow townsman, James Oswald of Dunnikier. Not only did Oswald become an intimate friend of Smith's, he was also the confidant, and, to some extent, the adviser of David Hume on economic matters. Oswald was an enlightened economist and both Hume and Smith gained much from discussions with him on economic matters. Although only eight years senior to Smith, Oswald had by 1750 made his mark in parliament by his deep understanding and appreciation of economic questions. David Hume is emphatic in his praise of Oswald, for in a letter to William Mure written in August, 1744, he says:

> I have past a week with Mr. Oswald at Kirkcaldy. He makes his compliments to you. He has shown me the whole economy of the navy, the source of the navy debt; with many other branches of public business. He seems to have a great genius for these affairs; and I fancy, will go far in that way, if he perseveres.[104]

102. *Letters of David Hume*, II, 334.
103. *Ibid.*, pp. 334–336.
104. *Ibid.*, I, 58.

Additional evidence for the influence which Oswald exerted on Smith's economic thinking came from Dugald Stewart, who writes:

> I cannot help adding, that the result of Mr. Smith's specu-lations, respecting the component parts of *price,* although sufficiently accurate for our present purpose, is by no means unexceptionable in point of distinctness.
>
> It appears from a manuscript of Mr. Smith's, now in my possessions, that the foregoing analysis, or division was suggested to him by Mr. Oswald of Dunnikier. It is somewhat remarkable, that the very same division is hinted at by Sir William Petty, who states it as an impedi-ment to national prosperity, that taxes should be levied on lands alone, and not on land, stock, and labour.[105]

There can be little doubt that Smith's close intimacy with Hume and Hutcheson, and, to a lesser extent, with Oswald, exercised a powerful influence on his economic philosophy. The originality of many of Hume's ideas is unquestioned since he had few predecessors in Britain, and the Physiocrats and Turgot had not yet published in 1748–1752. Hume was both the perceptive anticipator of Adam Smith and his acute critic, and Smith benefited greatly from almost thirty years of close relationship with him, quite apart from the inspiration he drew from his old teacher, Francis Hutcheson.

---

105. Stewart, *op. cit.,* IX, 6.

PART TWO

ECONOMIC COMMENTARIES

CHAPTER I

DIVISION OF LABOR

The germ of Adam Smith's treatment of the economic advantages flowing from the division of labor is to be found in Hutcheson's works. The latter's Chapter IV, "The Different States of Man,"[1] is one of the sources from which Smith drew when developing his own thoughts on the subject. It seems possible that sections of this chapter were in Smith's mind when he wrote of the advantages of the organization of industry based on the division of labor.

After describing the state of liberty as one of peace and beneficence, bearing no resemblance to Hobbes's pessimistic concept of it as a state of war and violence, Hutcheson showed that the members of a community are indebted for the comforts of life to the friendly and reciprocal aid of fellow members.

> Nor need we other proofs here that this first state founded by nature is so far from being that of war and emnity, that it is a state where we are all obliged by the natural feelings of our hearts, and by many tender affections, to innocence and beneficence towards all.[2]

Introducing the concept of mutual co-operation into the natural state of liberty Hutcheson comments:

> In the first place, 'tis obvious that for the support of human life, to allay the painful cravings of the appetites, and to afford any of those agreeable external enjoyments

1. Hutcheson, *System of Moral Philosophy*, I, 280–292.
2. *Ibid.*, p. 281.

> which our nature is capable of, a great many external
> things are requisite; such as food, clothing, habitations,
> many utensils, and various furniture, which cannot be ob-
> tained without a great deal of art, and labour, and the
> friendly aids of our fellows.[3]

Expanding upon this theme, he goes on to show that it is
impossible for man to obtain by his own unaided efforts all
of the comforts and necessities of life.

> Again, 'tis plain that a man in absolute solitude, tho' he
> were of mature strength, and fully instructed in all our
> arts of life, could scarcely procure to himself the bare
> necessaries of life, even in the best soils or climates;
> much less could he procure any grateful conveniences.
> . . . The mutual aids of a few in a small family, may
> procure most of the necessaries of life, and diminish dan-
> gers, and afford room for some social joys as well as finer
> pleasures. The same advantages could still be obtained
> more effectually and copiously by the mutual assistance
> of a few such families living in one neighbourhood, as
> they could execute more operose designs for the common
> good of all; and would furnish more joyful exercise of our
> social dispositions.[4]

Hutcheson then proceeds to enlarge on this simple illustration and apply the principle outlined to larger and more
complex communities by sketching in outline the mutual
advantages which accrue to each individual member of
large societies which follow these principles, as opposed to
the disadvantages of a "Crusoe" type of community.

> Nay, 'tis well known that the produce of the labours of any
> given number, twenty, for instance, in providing the
> necessaries or conveniences of life, shall be much greater
> by assigning to one, a certain sort of work of one kind,
> in which he will soon acquire skill and dexterity, and to
> another assigning work of a different kind, than if each
> one of the twenty were obliged to employ himself, by
> turns, in all the different sorts of labour requisite for his

3. *Ibid.*, p. 287.
4. *Ibid.*, pp. 287–288.

subsistence, without sufficient dexterity in any. In the former method each procures a great quantity of goods of one kind, and can exchange a part of it for such goods obtained by the labours of others as he shall stand in need of. One grows expert in tillage, another in pasture and breeding cattle, a third in masonry, a fourth in the chace, a fifth in iron-works, a sixth in the arts of the loom, and so on throughout the rest. Thus all are supplied by means of barter with the works of complete artists. In the other method scarce anyone could be dextrous and skilful in any one sort of labour.[5]

As is invariably the case with Hutcheson's economic ideas and discussion, these are also succinctly and admirably expressed in his *Introduction to Moral Philosophy*:

For let us observe what's very obvious, that without society of a good many of our fellows, their mutual aids, and an intercourse of friendly offices, mankind could neither be brought to life nor preserved in it; much less could they obtain any tolerable convenient or pleasant condition of life. 'Tis plain too that no one has such strength that he could promise himself to conquer all such as he may desire to wrong or spoil, and all such enemies as he may raise up against himself by an injurious course of life.[6]

Another remark later in the same book adds force to his statement of this principle:

Without thus ensuring to each one the fruits of his own labours with full power to dispose of what's beyond his own consumption to such as are dearest to him, there can be no agreeable life, no universal diligence and industry; but by such insurance labours become pleasant and honourable, friendships are cultivated, and an intercourse of kind officers among the good: nay even the lazy and slothful are forced by their own indigence, to bear their share of labour. Nor could we hope, in any plan of polity, to find such a constant care and fidelity in magistrates,

5. *Ibid.*, pp. 288–289.
6. Hutcheson, *Introduction to Moral Philosophy*, p. 131.

as would compel all impartially to bear their proper shares
of labour, and make a distribution of the common acquisition in just proportion to the indigence or merits of the
several citizens, without any partial regards to their fa-
vourites. And could even this be obtained in fact, yet
the citizens could scarce have such confidence in their
magistrates' wisdom and fidelity, as would make their
diligence and labour so agreeable to them, as when they
are themselves to make the distribution of their profits,
according to their own inclinations, among their friends
or families.[7]

These extracts together with the next one indicate clearly
that Hutcheson had firmly anticipated Smith's claims for the
advantages which would flow to society from the extension
of the division of labor.

Larger associations may further enlarge our means of
enjoyment, and give more extensive and delightful exer-
cise to our powers of every kind. The inventions, experience, and arts of multitudes are communicated; knowledge
is increased, and social affections more diffused. Larger
societies have force to execute greater designs of more
lasting and extensive advantage. These considerations
abundantly show the necessity of living in society, and ob-
taining the aid of our fellows, for our very subsistence;
and the great convenience of larger associations of men
for the improvement of life, and the increase of all our
enjoyments.[8]

It is, of course, not claimed that Francis Hutcheson in
his writings and teaching originated the ideas about the
advantages of the division of labor. Indeed, in a footnote [9]
to the above passage he tells us that he is indebted to the
second book of Cicero's De Officiis for his ideas, and he
commends Cicero's exposition. Nevertheless, on the basis
of these extracts, it does seem likely that Adam Smith had
these sections of Hutcheson's writings very much in mind

7. Ibid., pp. 141–142.
8. System of Moral Philosophy, I, 289–290.
9. Ibid., p. 290.

when he wrote about the advantages of the division of labor applied to economic life. There can be no doubt that Hutcheson admirably anticipated Smith's claim for the economic advantages of the division of labor. Smith, however, explored new ground in the Glasgow *Lectures* and the *Wealth of Nations* when he linked the concept directly to the facts of contemporary industrial organization and life.

While there is no trace in the works of David Hume of a discussion of the division of labor, additional anticipation of Smith's exposition are to be found in Sir William Petty's *Political Arithmetic* [10] and Bernard de Mandeville's *Fable of the Bees*.[11] The latter was particularly influential on Smith, and Dugald Stewart credited Mandeville with having been Smith's inspiration.[12]

Even earlier contributions to the development of the concept were made by Xenophon, Aristotle, Cicero, Aquinas, and Luther. Although Adam Smith's explanation of the notion is justly famous since he made it into one of the cornerstones of economic thinking, it is not outstanding for originality. Nor is it a complete exposition of the concept as already adumbrated by his predecessors.

Only three advantages for the division of labor are adduced both in the Glasgow *Lectures* and in the *Wealth of Nations*.

> This great increase of the quality of work, which, in consequence of the division of labour, the same number of people are capable of performing, is owing to three different circumstances; first, to the increase of dexterity in every particular workman; secondly, to the saving of the time which is commonly lost in passing from one species of work to another; and lastly, to the invention of

10. Sir William Petty, *Political Arithmetic*, republished in George A. Aitken (ed.), *Later Stuart Tracts* (Westminster: Archibald Constable and Co., Ltd., 1903), p. 10.

11. *The Fable of The Bees*, ed. F. B. Kaye (Oxford: The Clarendon Press, 1924), I, 356–358; II, 141–142, 284, 325.

12. Stewart, *op. cit.*, VIII, 311, 323.

a great number of machines which facilitate and abridge labour, and enable one man to do the work of many.[13]

It is interesting to note in this regard that all three of these advantages are also to be found in the account on 'Art' in the *Encyclopédie*, 1751, p. 717.[14] The latter also contains an article on the manufacture of pins in eighteen separate operations.[15] In the Glasgow *Lectures* Smith made the same points more briefly.

> But again, the quantity of work which is done by the division of labour is much increased by the three following articles: first, increase of dexterity; secondly, the saving of time lost in passing from one species of labour to another; and thirdly, the invention of machinery.[16]

It is not the intention to engage in a detailed criticism of Smith's understanding of the conomic advantages of the division of labor; but it is rather strange that he did not include among its advantages that springing from the cooperation of persons living in different lands, which enables different kinds of production to be carried out in the places best suited to them.

Adam Smith's particular merit lies wholly in his placing the division of labor as the cornerstone of his subsequent economic analysis. It is this which constitutes his major achievement in respect of the division of labor. The *Wealth of Nations* opens on this note when he shows that opulence is immediately dependent upon the division of labor. In order to show that growth in the national product is the direct result of the application and extension of division of labor, he gives his famous example of the principle operating in a particular industry which leads directly to an increase in its total output.

13. *The Wealth of Nations*, I, 9.
14. *Ibid.*, n. 4.
15. *Lectures of Adam Smith*, p. 164.
16. *Ibid.*, pp. 165–166.

To take an example, therefore, from a very trifling manufacture; but one in which the division of labour has been
very often taken notice of, the trade of the pin-maker;
a workman not educated in this business (which the division of labour has rendered a distinct trade) not
acquainted with the use of the machinery employed in
it, (to the invention of which the same division of labour
has probably given occasion) could scarce, perhaps, with
his utmost industry, make one pin in a day, and certainly
could not make twenty. But in the way in which this
business is now carried on, not only the whole work is
a peculiar trade, but it is divided into a number of
branches, of which the greater part are likewise peculiar
trades. One man draws out the wire, another straights it,
a third cuts it, a fourth points it, a fifth grinds it at the top
for receiving the head; to make the head two or three
distinct operations; to put it on, is a peculiar business, to
whiten the pins is another; it is even a trade by itself to
put them into the paper; and the important business of
making a pin is, in this manner, divided into about eighteen distinct operations, which, in some manufactories, are
all performed by distinct hands, though in others the
same man will sometimes perform two or three of them.
I have seen a small manufactory of this kind where ten
men only were employed, and where some of them consequently performed two or three distinct operations. But
though they were very poor, and therefore but indifferently accommodated with the necessary machinery, they
could, when they exerted themselves, make among them
about twelve pounds of pins a day. There are in a pound
upwards of four thousand pins of a middling size. Those
ten persons, therefore, could make among them upwards
of forty-eight thousand pins in a day. . . . But if they
had all wrought separately and independently, and without any of them having been educated to this peculiar
business, they certainly could not each of them have
made twenty, perhaps not one pin in a day; that is,
certainly, not the two hundred and fortieth, perhaps not
the four thousand eight hundredth part of what they are
at present capable of performing, in consequence of a

proper division and combination of their different operations.[17]

Smith is clearly indebted to Hutcheson for his appreciation of the significance of this concept. Credit must be given to Hutcheson for first implanting the notion in Smith's mind when Smith attended Hutcheson's lectures at Glasgow University. Like so many other political and economic ideas, however, it was in the "air" of the period, and Smith owes as much to many of his predecessors as to Hutcheson for developing in his mind an awareness of the economic significance of the concept.

Nevertheless, Adam Smith is to be praised for grounding the whole structure of his economic analysis on this concept. In this respect he synthesized the ideas of his forerunners, added a characteristically crucial economic twist or two of his own, and so integrated into economic theory one of its most important and basic ideas.

17. *The Wealth of Nations*, I, 6–7.

CHAPTER II

NOTIONS ON VALUE

In this chapter no exhaustive attempt is made to analyze all the aspects of the treatment of value by each of the three men.[1] Rather attention is concentrated on each author's development and understanding of the twin strands of "scarcity" and "utility," the basic elements in modern value theory.

Francis Hutcheson's doctrines on value had come to him in direct line of descent from Pufendorf via Gershom Carmichael. Pufendorf's very compact treatment of value clearly emphasized the two basic elements of scarcity and usefulness, as the following quotations from his *De Officio Hominis et Civis Juxta Legem Naturalem Libri Duo* so clearly show.

> Of common value the foundation as such is that aptitude of the thing or the service, by which it can contribute something directly or indirectly to the necessities of human life, and to make it more comfortable or agreeable. Hence we usually call things that serve no *use* at all things of no value. Yet there are some things most useful for human life, upon which no definite value is understood to have been set, either because they do not admit of ownership, and necessarily so, or because they are unsuited for exchange, and hence withdrawn from trade, or because in trade they are never considered otherwise than as an addi-

1. For a very much fuller treatment, see H. M. Robertson and W. L. Taylor, "Adam Smith's Approach to the Theory of Value," *Economic Journal,* LXVII (June, 1957), 181–198.

tion to something else [e.g. the ether, the heavenly bodies, the ocean, sunlight, clear, pure air, the fair face of the earth, the wind and shade]. . . . For in this matter the necessity of the thing, or its exalted usefulness, are so far from always holding the first place, that we rather see men hold in lowest esteem the things with which human life cannot dispense. And this because nature, not without the singular providence of God, pours fourth a bountiful *supply* of them. *Hence an increase of value tends to be produced especially by scarcity.* . . . For articles in everyday use prices are raised especially when their *scarcity* is combined with *necessity or want.* . . . The opposites of these things usually lower the price. . . . Sometimes the common price is suddenly changed, according to the abundance or scarcity of purchasers, money, or wares. For scarcity of purchasers and money, and also abundance of wares, diminish the price. On the other hand, abundance of would-be purchasers and of money, and scarcity of wares raise the price. So too it tends to lower the price, if wares seek a purchaser.[2]

These fundamental elements of usefulness and scarcity were transmitted to Hutcheson by his immediate predecessor at Glasgow, Gershom Carmichael.[3] As has been related in the Introduction, Carmichael translated Pufendorf's *De Officio Hominis et Civis* from the Latin, and added a critical expository commentary in the form of footnotes. Hutcheson regarded Carmichael, "that worthy and ingenious man," as "the best commentator on the book" and his notes to be "of much more value than the text." [4] To Pufendorf's brief chapter on value, Carmichael added several notes which show great acuteness and a masterly grasp of the various fundamental elements of the value problem, e.g.:

2. Samuel von Pufendorf, *De Officio Hominis et Civis Juxta Legem Naturalem Libri Duo,* trans. Frank Gardner Moore (*The Classics of International Law,* ed. James Brown Scott) (New York: Oxford University Press, 1927), II, 70–73 (italics supplied).

3. See W. L. Taylor, "Gershom Carmichael: A Neglected Figure in British Political Economy," *The South African Journal of Economics,* XXIII, (Sept., 1955), 251 ff.

4. Hutcheson, *Introduction to Moral Philosophy,* p. v.

In general we may say that the value of goods depends on these two elements, their *scarcity*, and the difficulty of acquiring them. . . . Furthermore, *scarcity* is to be regarded as combining two elements, the number of those demanding, and the usefulness thought to inhere in the good or service and which can add to the *utility* or pleasure of human life.[5]

Hutcheson's treatment of value is very similar to Pufendorf's as sharpened and developed by Carmichael. His brief but excellent exposition of the subject received its fullest treatment in his *System of Moral Philosophy*,[6] but it is more concisely though less effectively expounded in the *Introduction to Moral Philosophy*.[7] In the former we read:

The natural ground of all value or price or some sort of *use* which goods afford in life; this is prerequisite to all estimation. But the prices or values in commerce do not at all follow the real *use* or importance of goods for the support, or natural pleasure of life. . . . When some aptitude to human life is presupposed, we shall find that the prices of goods depend on these two jointly, the *demand* on account of some *use* or other which many desire, and the *difficulty* of acquiring, or cultivating for human use.[8]

"Use" is defined by Hutcheson as

Not only a natural subserviency to our support, or to some natural pleasure, but any tendency to give any satisfaction, by prevailing custom or fancy, as a matter of ornament or distinction.[9]

He explained "difficulty of acquiring" in terms of scarcity as

Not only great labour or toil, but all other circumstances which prevent a great plenty of the goods or performances demanded. Thus the price is increased by the rarity or *scarcity* of the materials in nature, or such accidents

5. Gershom Carmichael, *De Officio* (2nd ed.; Edinburgh: R. and A. Foulis, 1724), p. 247 (italics supplied).
6. *System of Moral Philosophy*, II, 53–55.
7. *Op. cit.*, pp. 199–203.
8. *System of Moral Philosophy*, II, 53–54.
9. *Ibid.*, p. 54.

as prevent plentiful crops of certain fruits of the earth; and the great ingenuity and nice taste requisite in the artists to finish well some works of art, as men of such genius are rare. The value is also raised by the dignity of the station in which, according to the custom of a country, the men must live who provide us with certain goods, or works of art.[10]

Hutcheson summarized his analysis as follows:

When there is no *demand*, there is no price were the *difficulty* never so great; and were there no difficulty or labour requisite to acquire, the most universal *demand* will not cause a price; as we see in fresh water in these climates. Where the demand for two sorts of goods is equal, the prices are as the difficulty. Where the difficulty is equal, the prices are as the demand.[11]

In the *Introduction to Moral Philosophy* Hutcheson added to his general theory of value a further interesting refinement which had been foreshadowed by Pufendorf:

Other things of great use have no price, either because they are naturally destined for community, or cannot come into commerce but as appendages of something else, the price of which may be increased by them, though they cannot be separately estimated; or because some law natural or positive prohibits all buying or selling of them.[12]

Although Hutcheson's analysis of value is not outstanding for any marked advance in utility analysis, it was a forerunner of Marshall's well-balanced, dual, "both-blades-of-the-scissors" approach. Hutcheson emphasized, as did both Pufendorf and Carmichael before him, the vital relationships of scarcity and value and stressed that "some sort of use" must be "a natural ground of all value or price," understanding by "use" something very similar to the modern concept of utility.

David Hume's economic discussions do not contain any

10. *Ibid.*, pp. 54–55.
11. *Ibid.*, p. 54.
12. *Op. cit.*, p. 200.

comprehensive treatment of value. Some idea of his thinking on the subject can be obtained only from the few
scattered asides he makes in the course of his accounts of
other economic phenomena. He believed labor, including
intellectual labor, to be the great source of value, and he
adopted the principle that every person should, if possible,
enjoy the fruits of his own labor.

> Everything is sold to skill and labour; and where nature
> furnishes the materials, they are still rude and unfinished,
> till industry, ever active and intelligent, refines them from
> their brute state, and fits them for human use and con-
> venience.[13]

And again: "Everything in the world is purchased by labour; and our passions are the only causes of labour." [14]

To obtain a more comprehensive idea of Hume's thinking
on value, it is necessary to examine his views on price, which
are included in his "Discourse on Money." While he is fully
aware of the influence that scarcity exerts on price, his main
argument in this essay is directed towards explaining the
proposition that " 'tis of no manner of consequence, . . .
whether money be in greater or less quantity" in establishing a country's internal price structure. He summarized as
follows:

> It seems a maxim almost self-evident, that the prices of
> everything depend on the proportion between commodi-
> ties and money. . . . Encrease the commodities, they be-
> come cheaper; encrease the money, they rise in their
> value. As, on the other hand, a diminution of the former,
> and that of the latter have contrary tendencies. . . . It is
> the proportion between the circulating money, and the
> commodities in the market, which determines the prices.[15]

That Hume was also fully aware of how supply and de-

---

13. *Essays Moral, Political and Literary*, I, 203–204.
14. *Ibid.*, p. 293.
15. *Ibid.*, pp. 316–318.

mand influenced price and value is reinforced by the following extract from one of Turgot's letters to Hume.

> You remark that I am supposing that wages increase in proportion to taxes, and that experience proves the falsity of this principle: and you justly observe that it is not taxes, high or low, which determine the price of wages, but simply the relation of supply and demand.
>
> This principle has certainly never been disputed; it is the only principle which fixes at the time the price of all the things which have a value in commerce. But one must distinguish two prices, the current price, which is established by the relation of supply to demand, and the fundamental price, which, in the case of a commodity, is what the thing costs the workman.[16]

These passages illustrate that Hume's sketchy treatment of value, which included no analysis of utility, emphasized how scarcity affects value, especially in regard to money.

The most important economic section of Adam Smith's *Lectures* is to be found in the section entitled "Cheapness and Plenty," Part II, Division II.[17] The two opening sections of this division are entitled (by Edwin Cannan) "Of the Natural Wants of Mankind" and "That All the Arts Are Subservient to the Natural Wants of Mankind." Cannan indicates in his Introduction to the *Lectures* that there is nothing corresponding to these two sections at the beginning of, or later on in the *Wealth of Nations*, though almost all the other important sections of this part of the *Lectures* correspond to the opening chapters in the *Wealth of Nations:*

> It is not easy to explain why the first two sections were omitted from the *Wealth of Nations*, and the fact will be regretted by those who ask for a theory of consumption as a preliminary to the other parts of political economy.[18]

16. *Reflections of the Formation and the Distribution of Riches*, ed. W. J. Ashley (New York: The Macmillan Company, 1898), p. 107.
17. *Lectures of Adam Smith*, pp. 157–236.
18. *Ibid.*, p. xxvii.

In these sections Smith emphasized from the outset the demand or consumption side, but leaves this factor out of his treatment in the *Wealth of Nations*.

From the beginning of Division II of the *Lectures* ("Cheapness and Plenty") Smith linked this general subject, "the most proper way of procuring wealth and abundance," directly with the ideas of scarcity and plenty; and like Pufendorf and Hutcheson, but unlike his own later positive treatment in the *Wealth of Nations*, he introduced this basic concept into his explanation of the water-diamond paradox:

> It is only on account of the *plenty* of water that it is so cheap as to be got for the lifting; and on account of the *scarcity* of diamonds (for their real use seems not yet to to have been discovered) that they are so dear.[19]

While it is true that these two opening sections of the *Lectures* are, at most, only discussions of "wants and their satisfactions," their inclusion marks a most significant contrast with what often has not unreasonably been regarded to be the one-sided general emphasis on labor and production in the *Wealth of Nations*.

The discussion of natural price in the *Lectures* is very similar to the treatment in the *Wealth of Nations*. As regards market price, however, the *Lectures* give three determinants which are much more explicit in the emphasis placed on utility and scarcity than in the *Wealth of Nations*.

> The regulation of the market price of goods depends on the three following articles:—
>
> First, the demand, or need for the commodity. There is no demand for a thing of little *use*; it is not a rational object of desire.
>
> Secondly, the abundance or scarcity of the commodity in proportion to the need for it. If the commodity be scarce, the price is raised, but if the quantity be more

19. *Ibid.*, p. 157.

than is sufficient to supply the demand, the price falls. Thus it is that diamonds and other precious stones are dear, while iron, which is much more useful, is so much cheaper, though this, [i.e. the proportion between the value of precious stones and iron] depends principally on the last cause, viz:—

Thirdly, the riches or poverty of those who demand. cheaper, though this, [i.e. the proportion between the value of precious stones and iron] depends principally price.[20]

Though the *Lectures* do not expand this treatment the explicit presence of these ideas, the perceptive connection and lucid linkage of utility, scarcity, and demand (in the manner of Hutcheson and Carmichael) may be held to mark a certain contrast with the treatment devoted to this problem in the *Wealth of Nations*.

In Chapter VII of the *Wealth of Nations*, which deals with natural and market price, Smith states that market price is "regulated by the proportion between the quantity which is actually brought to the market, and the demand of those who are willing to pay the natural price." [21] No additional word of explanation or analysis of "demand" is given beyond that by "demand," "effectual demand," and not the "absolute" demand, according to which "a very poor person may be said in some sense to have a demand for a coach and six," [22] is understood. Thus, while Pufendorf, Carmichael, and Hutcheson placed scarcity in a crucial place in their analyses, Smith made no explicit reference to "use" or usefulness, and only implicitly included scarcity.

A competition will immediately begin among them, and the market price will rise more or less above the natural price, according as either the greatness of the *deficiency*, of the wealth and wanton luxury of the competitors, happen to animate more or less the eagerness of the

20. *Ibid.*, pp. 176-177.
21. *The Wealth of Nations*, I, 58.
22. *Ibid.*

competition. Among competitors of equal wealth and luxury the same *deficiency* will generally occasion a more or less eager competition, according as the acquisition of the commodity happens to be of more or less importance to them. Hence the exorbitant price of the necessaries of life during the blockade of a town or in a famine.[23]

These ideas of scarcity and utility are essential for a satisfactory treatment of value theory, yet Smith tended to turn away from them and place greater emphasis on the role of labor.

Smith's famous treatment of utility and value is to be found in Book I, Chapter IV, of the *Wealth of Nations* and continues through Chapters V, VI, and VII, with further comments in Book I, Chapter XI, Part II. Book I, Chapter IV is rounded off by an elaborate analysis of a labor standard of value. In this chapter, contrary to Pufendorf's and Hutcheson's emphases on "use" as being "a natural ground for all value," Smith maintained that value in "use" was not an essential element of exchange value.

> The word VALUE, it is to be observed, has two different meanings, and sometimes expresses the utility of some particular object, and sometimes the power of purchasing other goods which the possession of that object conveys. This may be called "value in use"; the other "value in exchange". The things which have the greatest value in use have frequently little or no value in exchange; and on the contrary, those which have the greatest value in exchange have frequently little or no value in use. Nothing is more useful than water: but it will purchase scarce any thing; scarce any thing can be had in exchange for it. A diamond on the contrary, has scarce any value in use; but a very great quantity of other goods may be frequently had in exchange for it.[24]

23. *Ibid.*, pp. 58–59.
24. *Ibid.*, p. 30. See also I, 172–175, where Smith, in discussing the prices of the precious metals, states that the demand for them arises partly from their utility, and partly from their beauty. He mentions the qualities of utility, beauty, and scarcity as the basis of the high prices they demand.

Thus, unlike his immediate predecessors, who placed the term and concept of scarcity in a central position in their treatments of value, Smith, in his additional remarks on this subject, includes the idea of scarcity only implicitly, but not explicitly.

Smith's predecessors Pufendorf, Carmichael, and Hutcheson meant by "use" something which is similar to the modern concept of utility, while Smith in the above passage meant by "use" some narrower, ethically tinged sense of utility in which diamonds have little or none.

It is of no little interest to note that several previous commentators have tended to assume that the broad influence of Hutcheson on Smith covered their ideas on value. Smith's distinguished biographer, John Rae, wrote that Hutcheson's "remarks on value contain what reads like a first draft of Smith's famous passage on value in use and value in exchange."[25] This passage is quoted approvingly by W. R. Scott, who adds, however:

> It should be noted that while Hutcheson emphasises the position of labour he does not make it the sole distinguishing characteristic of wealth, for he also adds the limitation of supply and appropriation—as for instance, 'the rarity or scarcity of the materials in nature etc.'"[26]

This is, of course, an absolutely fundamental addition by Hutcheson, especially as Hutcheson, in one of the quotations given earlier, relates scarcity to demand.

The textual comparisons suggest, however, that the differences between Hutcheson and Smith, as they stand, have far more fundamental implications than any similarities.[27]

25. *Life of Adam Smith* (London: Macmillan and Co., 1895), p. 14.
26. *Francis Hutcheson, His Life, Teaching and Position in the History of Philosophy*, p. 237.
27. See Robertson and Taylor, *op. cit.*, for a development of this point of view.

CHAPTER III

MONEY AND INTEREST

1. MONEY

Following the important discussion of the nature of value, Francis Hutcheson has an interesting section in the *System* treating money as standards both of value and of deferred payments, and as a medium of exchange. He is fully aware that before the value of commodities can be calculated, the commodities "must be reduced to some common measure on both sides":

> Such as equal to the value of so many days labour, or to such quantities of grain, or to so many cattle of such species, to such a measure or weight of certain fruits of the earth, to such weights of certain metals.[1]

He recognizes that such a standard must be generally acceptable, and he asserts that it will differ, according to what commodity is generally desired in different countries.

In developing his treatment he states what he believes to be the necessary qualities of the most perfect standard of value and of deferred payments.

> The qualities requisite to the most perfect standard are these; it must be something generally desired so that men are generally willing to take it in exchange. The very making any goods the standard will of itself give them this quality. It must be portable; which will often be the case if it is rare, so that small quantities are of great value.

1. *System of Moral Philosophy*, II, 55.

It must be divisible without loss into small parts, so as
to be suited to the values of all sorts of goods; and it must
be durable, not easily wearing by use, or perishing in its
nature.[2]

After showing the inadequacies of barter as a means of
exchange, and the defects of corn and of other commodities
to serve as a medium of exchange, he sketches the reasons
why the precious metals have been used as the common
measure for value.

'Tis plain therefore that when man found any use for
the rarer metals, silver and gold, in ornaments or utensils,
and thus a demand was raised for them, they would soon
also see that they were the fittest standards for commerce,
on all the accounts above-mentioned. They are rare, and
therefore a small quantity of them easily portable, is
equivalent to large quantities of other goods; they admit
any divisions without loss; they are neither perishable,
nor easily worn by use. They are accordingly made standards in all civilised nations.[3]

In the *Introduction to Moral Philosophy* he expressed
these ideas in more concise terms:

The goods which are made the standard, should have
these properties; first, they should be of high value, that
so small a portable quantity of them may be equal in
value to a great quantity of other things; again, they
should not be perishable, or such as wear much in use;
and lastly they should admit of all manner of divisions
without loss. Now these three properties are found only
in the two more rare metals, silver and gold; which therefore have been made the standards of commerce in all
civilised nations.[4]

Continuing his discussion in the *System*, Hutcheson proceeded to show that coinage had been introduced to over-
come the inconvenience of using metals by weight and by

2. *Ibid.*, pp. 55–56.
3. *Ibid.*, p. 56.
4. *Introduction to Moral Philosophy*, p. 201.

quantity; two methods which involve the inherent inconveniences of "one, the trouble of making exact divisions, the other the uncertainty as to the purity of the metal." [5] In expanding this idea, he criticized with praiseworthy awareness the economic fallacies embedded in the commercial system usually termed "mercantilism." "Trading nations cannot make the comparative value of their coin with respect to other goods, greater or less than the value of the metal, and of the easy workmanship of coinage." [6] And he went on: "Coin is ever valued as a commodity in commerce, as well as other goods; and that in proportion to the rarity of the metal, for the demand is universal." [7]

Enlarging upon this aspect he severely condemned governmental interference with the coinage or the export of precious metals.

> A law can only fix or alter the legal denominations of pieces or ounces; and thus indeed affect within the state, the legal claims formerly constituted in those denominations: but commerce will always follow the natural value.[8] The governors of a state which has no monopoly of silver and gold, may change the names of their coins, and cheat their subjects, or put them into a state of cheating each other in their legal demands: but in commerce coin will retain the natural value of the metal in it, with little variation.[9]

In a vivid piece of analysis Hutcheson traced the effects on the economy to be expected whenever the currency was arbitrarily debased.

> If the legal names of our crown pieces were doubled so that the ounce of silver were called ten shillings, the nominal price of all goods would rise as much.[10]

---

5. *System*, II, 57.
6. *Ibid.*
7. *Ibid.*
8. *Ibid.*
9. *Ibid.*, p. 58.
10. *Ibid.*, p. 59.

> 'Tis a fundamental maxim about coin, that its value in commerce cannot be varied by names, that prices of goods keep their proportion to the quantity of metal, and not to the legal names.[11]

He also investigated the effect on the value of currency of the production of precious metals.

> An increase of both metals by copious mines, naturally abates the value of both, without any change of names. And thus, properly speaking, the values of gold and silver are fallen within these two centuries above one half.[12]

Working from an extension of this type of analysis, Hutcheson concluded that

> the most invariable salary would be so many days labour of men, or a fixed quantity of goods produced by the plain inartificial labours, such goods as answer the ordinary purposes of life. Quantities of grain come nearest to such a standard.[13]

David Hume, in his discourse *Of Money,* refuted the "mercantilist" error which tended to confound money with wealth. Opening his discussion, he forcefully stated that money was but a medium of exchange and that the quantity of money in circulation, statically considered, was a matter of indifference.

> Money is not, properly speaking, one of the subjects of commerce; but only the instrument which men have agreed upon to facilitate the exchange of one commodity for another. It is none of the wheels of trade. 'Tis the oil which renders the motion of the wheels more smooth and easy.[14]
> It was a shrewd observation of Anacharsis the Scythian, who had never seen money in his own country, that gold

---

11. *Ibid.,* p. 60.
12. *Ibid.,* p. 62.
13. *Ibid.,* p. 62–63.
14. *Essays Moral, Political and Literary,* I, 309.

and silver seemed to him of no use to the Greeks, but to assist them in numeration and arithmetic.[15]

Hume gave a quite uncompromising statement of his view of this matter. It can be said that no one before him had stated the idea as clearly or as succinctly.

Unlike so many of his successors, he went on to deal with the dynamic aspects of changes in the volume of money in circulation. Previous writings on this topic had emphasized, but only to a relatively minor degree, that an increased volume of money would stimulate economic activity; no particularly lucid explanation, however, had been presented to explain the mechanism of change. Hume, however, after criticizing adversely the value to the community of banks and paper credit, developed a dynamic analysis, backed by some ingenious observations, of the effects of an increase in the volume of money on a country's economy. He maintained that such an increase would stimulate industry during the interval which necessarily occurs before the enhanced amount is sufficiently diffused to alter the whole framework of prices. He described the economic advantages that would flow from a slowly increasing quantity of money, and the concomitant gently rising price level. His form of dynamic analysis was far superior to the tenuous attempts, in the same direction, of his predecessors. The latter tended to emphasize the effects on the price level of an absolute increase in the quantity of money. In a masterly analytical passage, Hume clearly distinguished, perhaps for the first time in economics, the short run from the long run, and indicated the benefits that would flow from controlled inflation. In a loose sense, Hume's analysis of the effects of changes in the quantity of money may be said to be the source of all the different types of modern dynamic theories of monetary phenomena.

15. *Ibid.*, p. 312.

It was this assumption about *changes* in the absolute volume of money in existence that was of the greatest importance to the future development of monetary analysis.

> Since the discovery of mines in America, industry has encreased in all the nations of Europe, except in the possessors of those mines; and this may justly be ascribed, amongst other reasons, to the encrease of gold and silver. Accordingly we find, that, in every kingdom, into which money begins to flow in greater abundance than formerly, every thing takes a new face; labour and industry gain life; the merchant becomes more enterprising; the manufacturer more diligent and skilful; and even the farmer follows his plough with greater alacrity and attention.[16]

The reasons he offered to explain this consequential spurt in economic activity are worthy of detailed attention.

> To account, then, for this phenomenon, we must consider, that though the high price of commodities be a necessary consequence of the encrease of gold and silver, yet it follows not immediately upon that encrease; but some time is required before the money circulates through the whole state, and makes its effect be felt on all ranks of people.[17]

Next followed his acute description of the role of time in economic activity.

> At first, no alteration is perceived; by degrees, the price rises, first of one commodity, then of another; till the whole at last reaches a just proportion with the new quantity of specie, which is in the kingdom. In my opinion, *it is only in the interval or intermediate situation* between the acquisition of money and rise of prices, that the encreasing quantity of gold and silver is favourable to industry.[18]

From this analysis of inflation, it can be seen he realized that genuine benefits would accrue to the economy in the short period. He pointed out that an inflow of money would

16. *Ibid.*, p. 313.
17. *Ibid.*
18. *Ibid.* (italics supplied).

stimulate greater economic activity through the rejuvenatory effects of altering people's habits of life and consumption patterns.

The hypothetical illustrations which he used to prove the futility of increasing or decreasing the money supply of a nation, illustrations which were taken over by the classical economists, refer only to the long run.[19] His preoccupation with the role of time can be seen from the following quotation.

> It is of no manner of consequence, with regard to the domestic happiness of a state, whether money be in greater or less quantity. The good policy of the magistrate consists only in keeping it, if possible, still encreasing; because, by that means, he keeps alive a spirit of industry in the nation, and encreases the stock of labour, in which consists all real power and riches.[20]

The kernel of Hume's contribution to monetary theory lies in his description of the process of how national economic activity is best stimulated. Higher prices will not immediately follow an increased supply of money; beneficial lags would occur before the effects are felt throughout the whole economy.[21]

Although Hume clearly stated the beneficial effects flowing directly from a mildly rising price level, he did not disregard the long-run consequences of absolute changes in the quantity of money. He thought the results were important, since they could alter the habits and customs of the population. He maintained that

> the prices of every thing depend upon the proportion betwixt commodities and money, and that any considerable alteration on either of these has the same effect, either of heightening or lowering the prices. Encrease the commodities, they become cheaper; encrease the money,

19. *Ibid.*, pp. 321–323.
20. *Ibid.*, p. 315.
21. *Ibid.*, p. 313.

they rise in their value. As, on the other hand, a diminution of the former, and that of the latter, have contrary tendencies.[22]

Proceeding from this maxim, which he regarded as being almost self-evident, he concentrated his attention on the significant factors which lie behind the total supply of goods and money. He believed that prices depend

> not so much on the absolute quantity of commodities and that of money, which are in a nation, as on that of the commodities, which come or may come to market, and of the money which circulates. If the coin be locked up in chests, it is the same thing with regard to prices, as if it were annihilated; if the commodities be hoarded in magazines and granaries a like effect follows. As the money and commodities, in these cases, never meet, they cannot affect each other.[23]

These quotations show that Hume had grasped the significance of money as a circulating medium in relation to the general price level, as opposed to the effects of the absolute quantity of money in existence. "It is the proportion between the circulating money, and the commodities in the market, which determines the prices." [24]

Hume continued his exposition by explaining that while prices in Europe had risen at the most, four times, since the discovery of the West Indies, the quantity of money in circulation in Europe had risen much more. In view of this fact, the question may well be asked: Why have prices not risen to a much higher level? Hume grounded his answer in an important psychological observation which he integrated into his general economic analysis; namely, prices have not so risen because of an accompanying change in the customs and manners of the nation. Through the stimulus imparted by increased money supplies and the

22. *Ibid.*, p. 316.
23. *Ibid.*, pp. 316–317.
24. *Ibid.*, p. 318.

induced increase in economic activity, total real output has increased. Thus, the increased supplies of money have helped to "preserve the proportion between coin and commodities nearer the ancient standard." [25]

His unerring grasp of the essential components of the real strength of an economy led him to reject the "mercantilist" view that money is everything.

> Here we may learn the fallacy of the remark, often to be met with in historians, and even in common conversation, that any particular state is weak, though fertile, populous, and well cultivated, merely because it wants money. It appears, that the want of money can never injure any state within itself: For men and commodities are the real strength of any community. It is the simple manner of living which here hurts the public, by confining the gold and silver to few hands, and preventing its universal diffusion and circulation.[26]

Hume's aim was to discredit the prevailing fallacy that the total quantity of a nation's money supply was, in itself, of paramount importance. In doing so, he concentrated his attention on two factors in his analysis which remain today, of the utmost importance: "There are only two circumstances of any importance, namely, their gradual increase [of the precious metals] and their thorough concoction and circulation through the state." [27]

Hume's fifth essay, "Of the Balance of Trade," also reveals his attitude towards the question of money. In this essay he assails the "mercantilist" view that it is desirable for a nation to have a favorable balance of trade. He regards as a "groundless apprehension" the fear that if trade is in a state of imbalance, money will flow out of the country.

> I should as soon dread, that all our springs and rivers would be exhausted, as that money should abandon a

25. *Ibid.*
26. *Ibid.*, p. 319.
27. *Ibid.*, p. 320.

kingdom, where there are people and industry. Let us
carefully preserve these latter advantages; and we need
never be apprehensive of losing the former.[28]

Hume's penetrating theory of money distinguishes the
point of view of the people from that of the sovereign and
also differentiates the operation of the long-run monetary
mechanism from that of the short run. He consolidated
his ideas about money into an integrated monetary theory
and related it directly to foreign trade and economic motivation. As a result, his notions on money are an integral
part of his theories of commerce, wages, interest, and profits, as later chapters show.

Adam Smith added nothing of significance to these expositions of David Hume and Francis Hutcheson. In fact,
his analysis and discussion of money is much inferior to
Hume's. Chapter IV, Book I, and Chapter II, Book II, of
the *Wealth of Nations*—entitled "Of the Origin and Use of
Money" and "Of Money considered as a particular Branch
of the General Stock of the Society, or of the Expence of
Maintaining the National Capital," respectively—contain
Smith's discussion of monetary theory.

He begins by pointing out that metals have been selected
as a medium of exchange because they are of durable and
divisible nature. While it cannot be convincingly claimed
that Smith adopted these notions from Hutcheson, since
they were also outlined in the works of, for example,
Pufendorf, Locke, Law, Montesquieu, Cantillon, and Harris,
Smith's historical description of the origin and use of money
very closely follows Hutcheson's discussion of the subject.
Smith considers such facets of the question as the necessity
for coinage and the necessity on the part of the public
authorities to refrain from tinkering with the monetary
system. The kinship of Hutcheson's 'debasing' to Smith's
'defrauding' is surely significant in this respect.

28. *Ibid.*, p. 331.

Like Hutcheson, Smith considered money to be the representative of labor, although his discussion of economic valuation emphasizes with a much greater degree of force than Hutcheson's that labor is the real measure of the exchangable value of all commodities. "Labour was the first price, the original purchase-money that was paid for all things. It was not by gold or by silver, but by labour that all the wealth of the world was originally purchased." [29]

He was also aware that gold and silver fluctuate in their value, and he points out that since the discovery of the American mines, the value of money had greatly depreciated. "The discovery of the abundant mines of America, reduced, in the sixteenth century, the value of gold and silver in Europe to about a third of what it had been before." [30] And again: "The discovery of the abundant mines of America, seems to have been the sole cause of this diminution in the value of silver in proportion to that of corn." [31]

In another passage which closely recalls Hutcheson's method of treatment, Smith relates how the different metals became the standard money of different nations.

> In the progress of industry, commercial nations have found it convenient to coin several different metals into money; gold for larger payments, silver for purchases of moderate value, and copper, or some other coarse metal, for those of still smaller consideration.[32]

Just as Hume said of money that it "is none of the wheels of trade. 'Tis the oil which renders the motion of the wheels more smooth and easy," [33] Smith expresses the same idea:

> . . . the great wheel of circulation is altogether different from the goods which are circulated by means of it. . . .

29. *The Wealth of Nations*, I, 32–33.
30. *Ibid.*, 34.
31. *Ibid.*, 191.
32. *Ibid.*, 40.
33. *Essays Moral, Political and Literary*, I, 309.

> Money, therefore, the great wheel of circulation, the great
> instrument of commerce, like all other instruments of
> trade, though it makes a part and a very valuable part of
> the capital, makes no part of the revenue of the society
> to which it belongs; and though metal pieces of which it
> is composed, in the course of their annual circulation,
> distribute to every man the revenue which properly be-
> longs to him, they make themselves no part of that
> revenue.[34]

Smith's original contributions to the development of monetary theory were practically nil. Much more serious, however, was Smith's failure to appreciate the value of Hume's work in the field. Hume's most significant contri-bution to monetary theory was his discussion of the short-run consequences of an increased supply of money, an aspect of Hume's analysis that Smith completely neglected.

The more formal and less economically significant nature of the physical properties of money—to which nearly all of Smith's discussion is restricted—had been discussed at considerable length by a great many of Smith's contempor-aries and predecessors, including Francis Hutcheson. Smith took over these doctrines, and it is impossible to ascertain the influence Hutcheson's particular discussion exerted on him. Nevertheless, the Smithian discussion closely follows the Hutcheson tradition, though not in all respects.

Hume's theory of money is far more elegant, consistent, and refined than Hutcheson's: and while Smith's fairly commonplace discussion is superior to his teacher's in that it shows faint traces of Hume's more perceptive notions— and, to this extent, at least, benefited from Hume's work— his rather sketchy monetary analysis is characterized by a somewhat uncritical adoption of the current orthodoxy as exemplified by Hutcheson's thought on the subject.

34. *The Wealth of Nations*, I, 272–275.

2. RATE OF INTEREST

Francis Hutcheson's treatment of interest is of considerable significance. Böhm-Bawerk believed that Turgot was the first writer to try to explain scientifically the relationship of interest to capital.

> So far as my knowledge of economical literature goes, I am bound to consider Turgot as the first who tried to give a scientific explanation of originary interest and accordingly as the first economist who showed the full extent of the problem.[1]

Francis Hutcheson, however, attempted just such an explanation in his *System,* published some fourteen years before Turgot's *Reflexions sur la formation et la distribution des richesses.*[2] Morever, the central idea of Hutcheson's explanation of the rate of interest was probably first stated in his lectures at Glasgow in 1736–1737, some forty years or so before Turgot's work was published.

Hutcheson's discussion of interest in the *System of Moral Philosophy* is to be found mainly in Chapter 13, Book II, entitled the "Principal Contracts in a Social Life." After distinguishing between "beneficent" contracts and "onerous" contracts, he classifies "the loan for use without any price or hire, where the same individual goods are to be returned" as a "beneficent" contract, and the type of loan where "a price or hire is given," as an "onerous" contract.[3] He then

---

1. E.v. Böhm-Bawerk, *Capital and Interest, History and Critique of Interest Theories* (South Holland, Illinois: Libertarian Press, 1959; translated from the original publication of 1884 by George D. Huncke and Hans F. Sennholz), I, 39.

2. It was written in 1766 but not published until 1769–1770, The *Reflexions* appeared in the *Ephemerides du Citoyen,* the journal of the Physiocrats. Turgot gave them to the editor, Du Pont de Nemours, who was short of material at the time. Although appearing in the issues labeled November and December, 1769, they were not actually published till January, February, and April, 1770. See *Reflections on the Formation and Distribution of Riches,* ed. W. J. Ashley (New York: The Macmillan Company, 1898), p. viii.

3. *System of Moral Philosophy,* II, 65.

goes on to define interest as follows: "If this loan for consumption be for a certain price beside the restitution of
equal quantities, 'tis called lending for interest." [4]

Hutcheson states his theory of interest in the following
manner.

> In loan for consumption at a set price or interest, the
> lender claims not the same individual, but equal quanti-
> ties, and the price for the loan. Some goods bear natural
> fruits or increase, as lands, stocks, herds, gardens. The
> grant of these fruits naturally deserves a price or rent. [5]

After justifying the existence of interest he proceeded to
elaborate his theory.

> Tho' goods have no fruits or increase, yet if they yield
> great convenience in life, and have cost such labour or
> expence as would have acquired goods naturally fruitful,
> if the proprietor grants the use of them, he may justly
> demand a price, such as he would have had if he had
> employed his money or labour on goods naturally fruitful.
> This is the case in setting of houses.
>
> If in any way of trade men can make far greater gains
> by help of a large stock of money, than they could have
> made without it, 'tis but just that he who supplies them
> with the money, the necessary means of this gain, should
> have for the use of it some share of the profit, equal at
> least to the profit he could have made by purchasing
> things naturally fruitful or yielding a rent. This shows the
> just foundation of interest upon money lent, tho' it be not
> naturally fruitful. [6]

The moralist is ousted from subsequent statements when
the economist, bases his conclusions, not on "what ought
to be," but on the demand for and supply of the factors
influencing the interest rate. Hutcheson begins his analysis
by stating:

> The reasonable interest varies according to the state of
> trade, and the quantity of coin. In a country newly settled,

4. *Ibid.*, p. 66.
5. *Ibid.*, p. 71.
6. *Ibid.*

or but beginning to trade, where few hands and little money are employed that way, great profits are made by small sums; and as in such places more land-rents are purchased for any given sum than in countries flourishing in trade, and abounding with money; an higher interest is reasonable, and no man would lend except upon an high interest. The gain too made by any sum is so large, that traders or purchasers can afford to give it. When many hands and much wealth are employed in trade, as men can be supported by smaller gains in proportion upon their large stocks, the profit made upon any given sum employed is smaller, and the interest the trader can afford must be less.[7]

He then launches into a more interesting and significant part of the analysis:

As money grows plentier, and bears less interest in loans, more incline to purchases of lands than formerly; and this demand raises the rates of lands, so that smaller land rents can be obtained for any sum. Men are therefore contented with smaller interest than formerly when they could have got greater land-rents. They should be satisfied if it surpasses the annual profits or purchases, as much as compensates the greater troubles or hazards attending the loans: and thus it falls of course, without the force of laws.[8]

He regarded the influence of demand and supply in determining the rate of interest as being of paramount importance. "Laws too must follow these natural causes in settling the interest, otherways they will seldom have their effect, and be iniquitous." [9]

Hutcheson maintains that the chief use of arbitrarily fixed legal rates of interest was their ability to "settle the interest decreed by courts on many occasions, where there has been no agreement of the parties; and to prevent the extortions of some grasping wretches upon the incautious,

7. *Ibid.*, p. 72.
8. *Ibid.*, pp. 72-73.
9. *Ibid.*, p. 73.

or the distressed," but he was convinced that "prudent men will settle this point for themselves according to the natural causes." [10] He concludes that in a wholly agricultural state (a sort of closed economy) where little foreign trade is permitted, and where great increases of wealth in the hands of a few are barred, all interest might well be abolished. But, he continues "where the strength of a state depends on trade, such a law would be ruinous." [11]

In a masterly analytical passage, Hutcheson traces the results on the economy which would occur if the legal rate of interest were not allowed to follow its natural causes and influences.

> If the legal rate of interest is high in wealthy nations, where small gains are made upon any given sum employed in trade, traders will not borrow without abatement of interest, nor will men borrow for purchasing lands, when the annual rents of them are far below the interest. Moneyed men may first run upon purchases, and decline to lend upon smaller than the legal interest; but the demand for lands will soon raise their price, so that they shall get much smaller annual rents for a given sum; many will therefore accept of interest below the legal, but higher than the annual rents of land. If the legal interest is made too low, few will incline to lend; they will first attempt to purchase lands; if the price of them rise by the great demand, so that small annual profit is made this way, moneyed men will turn to trade and manufactures. Men not educated to such business, or who choose to live without business, will find active traders always fond of borrowing at higher than the legal interest, and will find ways by discount, and annual gifts agreed upon, to elude the law.[12]

In the *Introduction to Moral Philosophy* Hutcheson restated with greater clarity the ideas previously embedded

10. *Ibid.*, pp. 73-74.
11. *Ibid.*, p. 74.
12. *Ibid.*, p. 73.

in the text of the *System*, which was published in 1775, although written about twenty years before then.

> If the loan is not designed as a favour, there's a right to demand *interest*. Nor is it necessary to make interest lawful that the goods lent be naturally fruitful; for tho' money for instance yields no natural increase; yet as by it one may purchase such goods as yield increase; . . . 'tis but natural that for such valuable advantages accruing to us by the loan, we should give the owner of the money some price or recompence proportioned to them. The prohibition of all loans for interest would be destructive to any trading nation, tho' in a democracy of farmers, such as that of the Hebrews was, it might have been a very proper prohibition.
>
> The just interest of money is to be determined according to the quantity of wealth employed in trade. Where there's a small quantity of money in a nation, and consequently all goods very cheap, a great profit is made, by any small sums employed with foreigners. And therefor a great interest may well be paid. But where money is employed in trade, a smaller profit is made on each sum thus employed, as the prime cost of goods is high; and therefor a smaller interest can be afforded for it. If civil laws settling interest don't regard these natural causes, they will not have their effect.[13]

These quotations show that Francis Hutcheson based his theory of interest firmly on the possibility, always open to the owners of capital, to find an alternative "fructification" for their resources, by investing in rent-bearing land. He was aware, too, that the rate of interest will reflect the strength of the demand for, and the supply of, "loanable funds." When demand for money is high and the supply of funds to satisfy the demand is low, he realized that the rate of interest would itself be high.

Although not entirely free of "mercantilist" beliefs in maintaining that the rate of interest depended principally

---

13. *Introduction to Moral Philosophy*, p. 209.

on the quantity of money, he is much in advance of most of his contemporaries. His insistence that the legal rate of interest must be permitted to follow closely the movements of the natural rate, and the fact that he did not advocate the prohibition of interest—e.g., "where the strength of a state depends on trade, such a law [prohibition of interest] would be ruinous" [14]—show a sophisticated degree of economic reasoning which lifts his work to a higher plane than was usual at that time.

David Hume's *Political Discourses* present a far more penetrating, extensive, and acute analysis of the theory of interest. A low rate of interest, as a mechanism for helping to achieve lower production costs, was a cherished aim of many early English writers on political economy. Hume, however, did not believe that the state should reduce the rate of interest by legal action. He recognized that the rate of interest was the natural result of economic conditions, and that it could not be modified satisfactorily by 'fiat.'

Hume opened his essay, "Of Interest," by stating the generally accepted fundamental condition that a low rate of interest reflected the healthy prosperity of an economy. "Nothing is esteemed a more certain sign of the flourishing condition of any nation than the lowness of interest." [15] He goes on to state that the rate of interest is not wholly governed by the absolute quantity of money in existence, especially under static conditions. "Lowness of interest is generally ascribed to the plenty of money. But money, however plentiful, has no other effect, *if fixed*, than to raise the price of labour." [16]

After showing that for all practical purposes an increase in the absolute quantity of money of fifteen times, or even only a doubling of the quantity would have no result other than to raise prices, he admitted that while prices had risen

14. *System*, II, 74.
15. *Essays Moral, Political and Literary*, I, 320.
16. *Ibid.*

about four times since the discovery of America, and that the supply of money had increased even more, the rate of interest had not fallen by much more than half.

> The rate of interest, therefore, is not derived from the quantity of precious metals.[17]
> It is in vain, therefore, to look for the cause of the fall or rise of interest in the greater or less quantity of gold and silver, which is fixed in any nation.[18]

Having thus cleared the way for the development of his own ideas, Hume enumerated the three factors which he considered to govern the level of the rate of interest.

> High interest arises from *three* circumstances: A great demand for borrowing; little riches to supply that demand; and great profits arising from commerce. . . . Low interest, on the other hand, proceeds from the three opposite circumstances: A small demand for borrowing; great riches to supply that demand; and small profits arising from commerce: And these circumstances are all connected together, and proceed from the encrease of industry and commerce, not of gold and silver.[19]

To illustrate his theory, Hume describes the sociological changes which occur in an imaginary society as it ascends the scale of civilized development, from a state of savagery to one of an organized and propertied state. As gradual evolution occurs, inequality of property inevitably develops. Thus, those who own more land than they can personally cultivate will employ the landless. Landlords will become firmly established in power positions in the state and, as time goes on, the pursuit of pleasure will become their chief occupation. ". . . . the prodigals amongst them [landlords] will always be more numerous than the misers." [20]

In the type of state where there is only a landed class, frugality, that attribute which Adam Smith was fulsomely

17. *Ibid.*, p. 321.
18. *Ibid.*, p. 323.
19. *Ibid.*, p. 322.
20. *Ibid.*

to praise, is practically non-existent, while the number of borrowers is very high, so that the rate of interest is high in proportion. "The difference depends not on the quantity of money, but on the habits and manners which prevail. By this alone the demand for borrowing is encreased or diminished." [21] This passage shows the quality of Hume's perception, which enabled him to go behind the "veil of money" and look for the "real" factors which govern the determination of the rate of interest. Behind the aggregate money volumes of lending and borrowing he saw, and duly emphasized, the habits and customs of the people as being the determining factors.

Hume next proceeds to argue that the second factor, "the great or little riches to supply this demand," also depends on the habits of the people, and not on the absolute quantity of money in circulation.

> In order to have, in any state, a great number of lenders, it is not sufficient nor requisite, that there be a great abundance of the precious metals. It is only requisite, that the property or command of that quantity, which is in the state, whether great or small, should be collected in particular hands, so as to form considerable sums, or compose a great monied interest. [22]

In this way a concentration of lenders is encouraged and their actions in the marketplace lower the interest rate.

It was Hume's firmly held conviction that a well organized and industrious economy would encourage a greater degree of frugality than an agricultural economy, and increase the supply of "loanable funds." For this reason he praised the merchant who accumulated funds, and condemned the land owners who dissipated their capital by borrowing for consumption purposes. He thought that their

21. *Ibid.*, p. 323.
22. *Ibid.*

actions tended to exhaust the national reserves of capital, and force up the interest rate charged on productive loans.

> Without commerce, the state must consist chiefly of landed gentry, whose prodigality and expence make a continual demand for borrowing; and of peasants, who have no sums to supply that demand. . . . Commerce alone assembles money into considerable sums; and this effect it has merely from the industry, which it begets, and the frugality which it inspires, independent of that particular quantity of precious metal which may circulate in the state.[23]

He considered that increased saving would be advantageous for the community, since this would stimulate an increase in the number of lenders and result eventually in a lower rate of interest.

To what extent the "increase of commerce diminishes the profits arising from that profession" is the next point Hume examines. The low rates of interest tempt merchants to expand their businesses and thereby increase the competition for "loanable funds"; this in turn leads to a decrease in the rates of profits.

> The low profits on merchandize induce the merchants to accept more willingly of a low interest, when they leave off business . . . . it is needless, therefore, to inquire which of these circumstances, *viz., low interest or low profit* is the cause, and which the effect? They both arise from an extensive commerce, and mutually forward each other. No man will accept of low profits, where he can have high interest; and no man will accept of low interest, where he can have high profits. An extensive commerce, by producing large stocks, diminishes both interest and profit, and is always assisted, in its diminution of the one, by the proportional sinking of the other.[24]

Hume employs a wealth of historical detail to illustrate his conception of the relationship between the quantity of

23. *Ibid.*, p. 326.
24. *Ibid.*, p. 327.

money and the rate of interest. He maintains that those who assert that a large quantity of money is the cause of low interest have "taken a collateral effect for a cause." [25] He argues that revitalized industries and general increased economic activity in the economy, which have caused the reduction in the interest rate, have also led to increased supplies of money. He does not categorically deny that the size of the money supply is wholly unimportant in determining the rate of interest, but he couples its influence with the reason given above. "But though both these effects, plenty of money and low interest, naturally arise from commerce and industry, they are altogether independent of each other." [26]

He puts forward two solutions—one applicable to Spain and the other applicable to England and France—in his attempt to grapple with this problem. In Spain the first effect of the increased money supply following the discovery of the New World was to halve the interest rates. Does this fact invalidate Hume's contention that interest is independent of the absolute size of a country's money supply? Prima facie it seems to.

> The causes of the sinking of interest, upon such an event, seem different in the conquering country and in the neighboring states; but in neither of them can we justly ascribe that effect merely to the encrease of gold and silver.[27]

He admits that it seems natural in a conquering country for new money to become concentrated in a few hands, so that the same effect is obtained by the increase of money as is produced by the increase in commerce, and that lenders will exceed borrowers, and so tend to depress interest rates. But he also points out that after the influx of new money has been absorbed in the economy, conditions will soon return to their previous state. That is, the landlords and new

25. *Ibid.*
26. *Ibid.*, p. 328.
27. *Ibid.*, p. 329.

money holders will gradually squander their newly acquired wealth, so that the net effect will be increased prices brought about by the increased supply of money, which is redistributed throughout the economy. It is no longer held in large reserves, and "the disproportion between the borrowers and lenders is the same as formerly, and consequently the high interest returns." [28]

The position, on the other hand, in England and France and the other European countries which did not possess mines was different from that in Spain. Interest reductions in these countries did not spring only from an increase in money, since interest reduction had been gradual and had been caused primarily by the increase in economic activity, engendered in the short period between the increase in the money supply and the consequent rise in prices.

Hume's theory of interest was a frontal attack on the contemporary doctrine that the rate of interest depended basically on the supply of money. His theory foreshadowed that which later emerged, conceiving of interest as being dependent on the supply of capital in relation to its demand. His theory, by distinguishing money used as capital from money used on consumption, contained the germ of the modern ideas of consumption and investment. Hume's insistence, too, on the part played by the habits and customs of the people anticipated much of the subsequent thought of the German Historical School, and the Veblen Institutionalists.

Although his work was a mixture of ideas suggested by some of his predecessors, he accomplished something quite new when he grounded it in national habits and customs, and the fundamental principles of economic motivation. His analytical skill enabled him to separate essential ideas from the superfluous and weave a well-rounded, integrated theory of his own.

28. *Ibid.*

Adam Smith's remarks on interest theory are located chiefly in Book I, Chapters VI, VIII, IX, and Book II, Chapter IV, of the *Wealth of Nations,* and also in the *Lectures,* pages 219–220. In the latter Smith begins by stating the usually accepted doctrine of his time. "It is commonly supposed that the premium of interest depends on the value of gold and silver."[29]

In the *Wealth of Nations* this common opinion was attributed to Locke, Law, and Montesquieu, who taught that the increase in the quantity of money following the discovery of the New World caused the lowering of the interest rate in Europe.[30] Smith noted that Hume had so fully exposed the fallacy inherent in this reasoning that he hardly considered it worthwhile to say anything more on the subject.[31] However, he included both in the *Lectures* and in the *Wealth of Nations* short passages illustrating the fallacy inherent in the earlier reasoning about the matter.

> The value of these [gold and silver], are regulated by their quantity, for as the quantity increases, the value diminishes, and as the quantity decreases, the value rises. If we attend to it, however, we shall find that the premium of interest is regulated by the quantity of stock.[32]

The word "stock" contains the clue to Smith's treatment of interest.

> The stock which is lent at interest is always considered as a capital by the lender. He expects that in due time it is to be restored to him, and that in the meantime, the borrower is to pay him a certain annual rent for the use of it. The borrower may use it either as a capital, or as a stock reserved for immediate consumption. If he uses it as capital, he employs it in the maintenance of productive labourers, who reproduce the value with a profit. . . . If he uses it as a stock reserved for immediate consumption, he acts the

29. *Lectures of Adam Smith,* p. 219.
30. *The Wealth of Nations,* I, 335.
31. *Ibid.*
32. *Lectures,* pp. 219–220.

part of a prodigal, and dissipates in the maintenance of the idle, what was destined for the support of the industrious.[33]

Continuing the discussion Smith describes what he means by the real nature of interest.

Almost all loans at interest are made in money, either of paper, or of gold or silver. But what the borrower really wants, and what the lender really supplies him with, is not the money, but the money's worth, or the goods which it can purchase. . . . By means of a loan, the lender, as it were, assigns to the borrower his right to a certain portion of the annual produce of the land and labour of the country, to be employed as the borrower pleases.[34]

The same point had been made years before in the *Lectures*.

No doubt it is generally money which one man delivers another in a loan, but then it is immediately turned into stock, and thus the quantity of stock enables you to make a greater number of loans.[35]

Smith concluded that the quantity of stock, which was usually expressed as the quantity of money which can be lent at interest in any country, was independent of the value of money, but dependent on

the value of that part of the annual produce which . . . is destined not only for replacing a capital, but such a capital as the owner does not care to be at the trouble of employing himself. As such capitals are commonly lent out and paid back in money, they constitute what is called the monied interest.[36]

Continuing from this point Smith observes that "as stock increases, the quantity of stock to be lent at interest grows gradually greater and greater." [37]

33. *Wealth of Nations*, II, 332.
34. *Ibid.*, p. 333.
35. *Lectures*, p. 220.
36. *Wealth of Nations*, II, 333.
37. *Ibid.*, p. 335.

He argues that as this process occurs, the interest rate decreases through the influence of the following mechanism.

> As capitals increase in any country, the profits which can be made by employing them necessarily diminish. It becomes gradually more and more difficult to find within a country a profitable method of employing any new capital. There arises in consequence a competition between different capitals, the owner of one endeavouring to get possession of that employment which is occupied by another. . . . Their competition raises the wages of labour, and sinks the profits of stock. But when the profits which can be made by the use of a capital are in this manner diminished, as it were, at both ends, the price which can be paid for the use of it, that is, the rate of interest must necessarily be diminished with them.[38]

This element in his exposition sounds remarkably like the Keynesian concept of the "falling marginal efficiency of capital." Thus, according to Smith, the rate of interest falls as capital increases and as profits fall, because of the competition arising between investors. This element is not mentioned in the *Lectures*. There Smith had only this to say:

> If there be few who have it in their power to lend money, and a great number of people who want to borrow it, the price of interest must be high; but if the quantity of stock on hand be so great as to enable a great number to lend, it must fall proportionably.[39]

Smith defined interest as the revenue

> derived from stock by the person who does not employ it himself, but lends it to another. . . . It is the compensation which the borrower pays to the lender, for the profit which he has an oppuortunity of making by the use of the money. Part of that profit naturally belongs to the borrower, who runs the risk and takes the trouble of employing it; and part to the lender, who affords him the opportunity of making this profit. The interest of money

38. *Ibid.*
39. *Lectures*, p. 220.

is always a derivative revenue which, if it is not paid from the profit which is made by the use of money, must be paid from some other source of revenue, unless perhaps, the borrower is a spendthrift, who contracts a second debt to pay the interest of the first.[40]

Smith's role was to blend theories previously enunciated. Essentially, he studied the question as a problem in price theory and stated that interest was necessary in order to produce a sufficient supply of capital.

> Something must be given for the profits of the undertaker of the work who hazards his stock in this adventure. . . . He could have no interest to employ them [workmen], unless he expected from the sale of their work something more than what was sufficient to replace his stock to him.[41]

It was necessary that a sufficient supply of capital should be accumulated because of the need to advance loans to the large numbers of people who depended, directly or indirectly, on the accumulation of capital and its eventual employment for the necessities of life.

> In all arts and manufactures the greater part of the workmen stand in need of a master to advance them the materials of their work, and their wages and maintenance till it be completed.[42]

To the question of whether or not interest can be justified, Smith expressed his opinion in a wonderfully simple way: "But as something can every where be made by the use of money, something ought every where to be paid for the use of it." [43]

Obviously, Smith did not overlook the problem of interest, but he did not give a completely satisfactory answer to the question. The explanation of natural interest which im-

40. *Wealth of Nations*, I, 54.
41. *Ibid.*, p. 50.
42. *Ibid.*, p. 67.
43. *Ibid.*, p. 338.

pressed him most amounted to the statement that there must be a profit in capital; otherwise entrepreneurs would have no reason for employing capital in productive undertakings.

Traces of Francis Hutcheson's ideas, and also traces of Hume's theory, reappear in Smith's discussion of the subject. Smith had almost disregarded the normative terminology that ran through Hutcheson's work. He replaced it, to some extent, with the acute subtlety of thought characteristic of so much of Hume's treatment of economic topics. Smith's treatment, however, is not entirely free of normative overtones, e.g.: "But as something can everywhere be made by the use of money, something ought everywhere to be paid for the use of it." [44]

Hutcheson maintained that the rate of interest depended on two factors, "the state of trade [demand], and the quantity of coin [supply]," [45] or more explicitly, "on the quantity of wealth employed in trade." [46] Generally speaking, he assumed that the supply of and the demand for money were the crucial factors to be considered. He was not unaware of the roles played by the level of economic activity and the ratio of commercial profits to money invested, but he tended to emphasize, as the determining factor, the absolute size of the nation's money supply. Smith and Hume developed both factors, but recognized the paramount place of the level of economic activity.

Hume rendered the very important service to economics of showing the erroneousness of the idea that the rate of interest depended only on a nation's quantity of money. He illustrated that the reduction of interest must, in general, be the result of "the increase of industry and frugality of arts and commerce." [47] In the more formal parts of his analysis, a gem of perspicuity and stimulating thought, he concen-

44. *Ibid.*
45. *System*, p. 338.
46. *Introduction to Moral Philosophy*, p. 209.
47. *Essays Moral, Political and Literary*, I, 327.

trated on the influence of the three factors which he considered to determine the rate of interest. To the demand and supply analysis of capital, he added the third factor, viz., profits arising from commerce.

An essential, cohesive strand in his analysis was his lavish praise of the virtues of the merchant class. He saw the merchants, by the dint of frugality and parsimony, accumulating large reserves of money which exercised a depressive influence on the rate of interest. These reserves could not be created if trade was languid. Thus, low profits and low interest are brought about by the same cause—the flourishing state of the economy. In Hume's analysis the chief influence is attributed to the frugality of the merchant class, who by their parsimonious habits provide the funds for the expansion of internal and external trade.

This kind of discussion reappeared in the work of Smith, who developed a more realistic definition of interest than either Hutcheson or Hume. He is more concerned with the "real" factors, and he defined interest as a command over "real" resources. He wholeheartedly accepted Hume's thesis that the rate of interest depended upon the state of trade, the rate being low when trade was healthy, but he refined Hume's analysis of the demand and supply of money into the demand and supply of "loanable funds."

Smith explained that as stock as a whole increased, then that part of the stock—the supply to be lent at interest—must also increase. The supply of stock could be increased only by refraining from current consumption, and here we see Hume's central concept assuming the major role in Smith's argument. As this increase in stock developed, interest would decrease for two reasons. First, because the supply of "loanable funds" had increased, and second, and more important, because the "marginal efficiency of capital" had fallen.[48] Hence, it is apparent that Adam Smith's

48. *Wealth of Nations*, I, 335.

theory of interest owed much to Hutcheson and Hume—
more, however, to Hume, who provided the stimulus for
Smith's doctrine of parsimony, but not for its extreme one-
sidedness.

CHAPTER IV

LUXURY AND PARSIMONY

A widely held doctrine in the first half of the eighteenth
century maintained that national economic policy directed
towards the prevention of the purchase of luxury goods, acting in conjunction with measures designed to boost the level
of savings, would be detrimental to the prosperity of the nation and to the particular interests of labor.

It was a common assumption that the level of total employment varied closely with the level of total expenditure
on luxuries, especially on home-produced luxuries. Bernard
Mandeville's *Fable of the Bees*, with its morally shocking
doctrine of "private vice-publick benefits," cynically defended this point of view. Mandeville recognized clearly that
there was an important problem in maintaining a high level
of aggregate demand.[1] Purely morally, there was severe
condemnation of Mandeville's reliance on 'vicious' luxury
expenditure in the midst of mass poverty in order to stimulate and maintain employment.[2] Apart, however, from the
many moral criticisms of Mandeville's thesis—which anticipated Keynes in recognizing that expenditure by the
rich may create employment—several writers, including

1. *The Fable of the Bees: or, Private Vices, Publick Benefits*, ed. F. B.
Kaye.
2. See T. W. Hutchison, "Berkeley's *Querist* and Its Place in the Economic
Thought of the Eighteenth Century," *The British Journal for the Philosophy
of Science*, IV (1953), 52.

Berkeley, Petty, and Stewart, wholeheartedly accepted his economic doctrine, with the qualification that luxury expenditure on imports was not beneficial to the nation.[3] There was general agreement, though, that expenditure on home-produced luxuries promoted the economic welfare of labor and of the country.

Like most of his contemporaries, Francis Hutcheson was morally opposed to Mandeville's doctrine of the encouragement of luxury expenditure. What was more significant, however, for the future course of economic thought, was Hutcheson's opposition to the economic analysis on which the doctrine rested. He believed that "income not spent in one way will be spent in another and if not wasted in luxury will be devoted to useful prudent purposes."[4]

In criticizing Mandeville's economic analysis Hutcheson set out to prove that

> if it can be made to appear that there may be an equal consumption of manufactures without these vices, and the evils which flow from them; that wealth and power do not naturally tend to vice, or necessarily produce it; then, though we allow that these vices do consume manufactures and encourage industry in the present consumption of manners, and that these vices often attend wealth and power, yet it will be unjust to conclude, either that *vices naturally tend to public prosperity or are necessary to it; or that public happiness does necessarily occasion them.*[5]

He continued his critique by remarking that "good arising to the public, is in no way owing to the luxurious, intem-

3. See George Blewitt, *An Enquiry whether a General Practice of Virtue tends to the Wealth or Poverty, Benefit or Disadvantage of a People* (London, 1725), p. 40, for typical opposition to Mandeville's inclusion of luxury expenditure on imports in his general scheme. See also Edgar S. Furniss, *The Position of the Laborer in a System of Nationalism* (New York: Kelley and Millman, Inc., Reprints of Economic Classics, 1957), for a brilliant discussion of mercantilist ideology. This book was first published in 1920.

4. T. W. Hutchison, *op. cit.*, p. 71.

5. F. Hutcheson, *Reflections upon Laughter and Remarks upon the Fable of the Bees* (Glasgow: R. and A. Foulis, 1750), pp. 55–56.

perate or proud but to the industrious, who must supply all customers." [6]

Hutcheson did not accept the beneficial effect of expenditure on luxury goods, and he formulated the completely opposite economic analysis that aggregate effective demand would be satisfactorily attained if luxury expenditure was not encouraged:

> Unless therefore all mankind are fully provided not only with all the necessaries, but all innocent conveniences and pleasures of life, it is still possible without any vice, by an honest care of families, relations, or some worthy persons in distress, to make the greatest consumption. [7]

Having stated in forthright terms his uncompromising opposition to the Mandevillian thesis, Hutcheson proceeded to illustrate his position and ridicule his opponent's idea by concentrating his criticism on one of Mandeville's more strained illustrations.

> Who needs be surprised that luxury or pride are made necessary to public good, when even theft and robbery are supposed by the same author [Mandeville] to be subservient to it, by employing locksmiths? Not to repeat again, that all the good effect is plainly owing to the industrious, and not to the robber; were there no occasion for locks, had all children and servants discretion never to go into chambers unseasonably, this would make no diminution of manufactures; *the money saved to the housekeeper would afford either better dress, or other conveniences to a family, which would equally support artificers,* even smiths themselves might have equal employment. Unless all men be already so well provided with all sorts of convenient utensils, or furniture, that nothing can be added, a necessity or constant usefulness of robbers can never be pretended, any more than the public advantages of shipwrecks and fires, which are not a little admired by the author of the fable. [8]

6. *Ibid.*, p. 60.
7. *Ibid.*, p. 63.
8. *Ibid.*, pp. 64–65 (italics supplied).

In passages like these Hutcheson voiced his disagreement with the doctrine that expenditure on luxury goods is beneficial to the community. He advanced, in apparently harmless terms, the genesis of the opposite economic doctrine, which later assumed that the forces of demand and supply were usually self-adjusting. The eventual outcome of this kind of analysis culminated in the pre-Keynesian "Treasury-view" that public works expenditure would not help to diminish total unemployment, and to the rejection of all "under-consumptionist" doctrines.

Hume, on the other hand, once again illustrating his well-rounded and acute analytical powers accepted the economic arguments of Berkeley, Barbon, and Mandeville. In his "Discourse on Luxury" Hume commented that

> the ages of refinement and luxury are both the happiest and most virtuous; secondly, that where ever luxury ceases to be innocent, it also ceases to be beneficial, and when carried a degree further, is a quality pernicious, to political society.[9]

He was convinced that

> the increase and consumption of all the commodities, which serve to the ornament and pleasure of life, are advantageous to society; because, at the same time that they multiply those innocent gratifications to individuals, they are a kind of *storehouse* of labour, which, in the exigencies of the state, may be turned to public service. In a nation, where there is no demand for such superfluities, men sink into indolence, lose all enjoyment of life, and are useless to the public, which cannot maintain nor support its fleets and armies, from the industry of such slothful members.[10]

He was appreciative of the influence exerted on the level of aggregate demand by the demand for luxuries:

> Luxury, when excessive, is the source of many ills; but is in general preferable to sloth and idleness. . . . By banish-

9. *Essays Moral, Political and Literary*, I, 307.
10. *Ibid.*, pp. 302–303.

ing *vicious* luxury, without curing sloth and an indifference to others, you only diminish industry in the state, and add nothing to men's charity or their generosity.[11]

These quotations show that Hume recognized that expenditure on luxury commodities, far from being a moral and economic sin, was of direct economic benefit to the nation as a whole. Hume believed that the creation of new wants, together with the efforts made to satisfy them would stimulate industry to produce the new goods and services which had not previously been an integral part of the community's consumption pattern, and lead to increased economic activity, and an increase in the wealth of the nation.

> And to consider the matter abstractly, manufacturers encrease the power of the state only as they store up so much labour, and that of a kind which the public may lay claim without depriving any one of the necessaries of life. The more labour, therefore, is employed beyond mere necessaries, the more powerful is any state. . . . In a state without manufacturers, there may be the same number of hands; but there is not the same quantity of labour, nor of the same kind. All the labour is there bestowed upon necessaries, which can admit little or no abatement.[12]

Hume was not prepared to accept complacently the traditional low standard of living, which prevailed among the members of the laboring classes. He recognized that the employment of laborers in the production of luxuries would help to increase the level and intensity of effective demand. He also saw that it would decrease unemployment and help to inculcate a desirable habit of industry, and so help break the seemingly inevitable circle of pauperism and "sloth."

> Thus the greatness of the sovereign and the happiness of the state are, in a great measure, united with regard to trade and manufactures. It is a violent method, and in most

11. *Ibid.*, pp. 308–309.
12. *Ibid.*, p. 294.

cases impracticable, to oblige the labourer to toil, in order to raise from the land more than what subsists himself and family. Furnish him with manufactures and commodities, and he will do it himself.[13]

His unflagging concern with the problem of raising the standard of living—a concern not unanimously displayed by writers of this period—but supported by Dudley North,[14] George Berkeley,[15] and Sir James Steuart,[16] is further illustrated by his appeal for a general increase of "real" wages.

Every person, if possible, ought to enjoy the fruits of his labour, in a full possession of all the necessaries, and many conveniences of life. No one can doubt, but such an equality is most suitable to human nature, and diminishes much less from the *happiness* of the rich than it adds to that of the poor.[17]

He believed that high "real" wages were desirable because they tended to lift the level of employment and demand, and should not be discouraged, even if they were thought to affect adversely the balance of foreign trade.

In this circumstance [the presence of high "real" wages] consists the great advantage of England above any nation at present in the world, or that appears in the record of any story. It is true, the English feel some disadvantage in foreign trade by the high price of labour, which is in part the effect of the riches of their artisans, as well as of the plenty of money: But as foreign trade is not the most material circumstance, it is not to be put in competition with the happiness of so many millions.[18]

Adam Smith was completely familiar with the economic doctrines of Hume, Mandeville, Berkeley, and Hutcheson,[19]

13. *Ibid.*
14. Dudley North, *Discourses upon Trade* (London: 1691), p. 27.
15. George Berkeley, *The Querist* (5th ed.; Dublin: 1750), pp. 3–12.
16. Sir James Steuart, *An Inquiry into the Principles of Political Oeconomy* (London: 1767), I, 62–65.
17. *Essays Moral, Political and Literary*, I, 296–297.
18. *Ibid.*, p. 297.
19. See James Bonar, *A Catalogue of the Library of Adam Smith* (2nd ed.; London: Macmillan and Co., 1932), pp. 84, 90 and 91.

to name but a few of the participants in the "private vice-publick benefits" controversy. But Smith did not accept Mandeville's economic argument. On the contrary, Smith built on Hutcheson's assumptions, and rejected the assumption that aggregate demand could be too low.[20]

Adam Smith very strongly disapproved of luxury expenditure, and praised the virtues of public and private savings with an enthusiasm not exceeded by any of his leading predecessors or contemporaries. He developed the economic analysis that saving *is* investment, "that if people do not spend their money in one way they will spend it in another,"[21] and based on this view his warm praise of the virtues of parsimony. His optimistic opinion of human nature—his view that self-interest and laissez-faire coincided in a beneficial manner for the good of the state and the individual—led him to conclude that effective demand could be left to find its own necessarily advantageous level, without the need for state intervention. He believed private and public parsimony to be economically advantageous to the state and its inhabitants, and that consequently, the utmost thrift and economy should be practiced by the state and the individual.

Smith received the germs of this doctrine from Francis Hutcheson, who maintained that the level of aggregate effective demand could be adequately attained without expenditure on luxury consumption. Hume's eminently well-balanced presentation of the economic argument carried no weight at all with Smith. This Hutchesonian influence became the basis for Smith's vastly influential economic analysis of saving and investing. It ultimately became the authoritative doctrine which succeeded in establishing itself as the true orthodoxy, and led to the eventual rejection of the later unorthodox "underconsumptionist" arguments.

20. See T. W. Hutchison, *op. cit.*, p. 72.
21. J. M. Keynes, *The General Theory of Employment Interest and Money* (London: Macmillan and Co., 1936), p. 20.

Adam Smith did not recognize that under certain conditions the state can, by employing various economic policy measures, maintain a level of demand sufficient to insure as full an employment of resources as is consistent with the abolition of the paradox of poverty in the midst of plenty. To Smith and his traditional followers full employment was not the vital problem and preoccupation it had been with most of his British predecessors and contemporaries. As J. A. Schumpeter has remarked:

> Chapter III of the *Wealth of Nations* (which introduces the distinction between productive and unproductive labour), with its tremendous emphasis on the propensity to save as the true creator of physical capital, marks the victory for more than 150 years to come of a pro-saving theory.[22]

In their attempts to abolish pauperism and widespread unemployment, eighteenth-century policy-framers who devised schemes to create employment came up against the seemingly perverse fact that an increase in wages, in real or in money terms, was almost always unfailingly followed by a fall in the total supply of labor. This irritating phenomenon had been observed by many authors in their study of actual labor conditions. That the more people were paid, the less they worked was a truth observed over and over again.[23]

> It is observed by clothiers and others, who employ great numbers of poor people, that when corn is extremely plentiful, that the labour of the poor is proportionably dear; and scarce to be had at all so licentious are they who labour only to eat, or rather to drink.[24]

Hume did not express his views on this subject in his usual distinctive manner, but he mentioned that there was an in-

22. Joseph A. Schumpeter, *History of Economic Analysis* (London: George Allen and Unwin, Ltd., 1954), p. 193.
23. Furniss, *op. cit.*, pp. 118 and 234–235.
24. Sir William Petty, *Political Arithmetic* (reprinted in *Later Stuart Tracts*, ed. George A. Aitken; Westminster: Archibald Constable and Co., Ltd., 1903), p. 31.

crease in the number of working days in periods of scarcity,
but not in periods of abundance:

> 'Tis always observed, in years of scarcity, if it be not ex-
> treme, that the poor labour more, and really live, better
> than in years of great plenty, when they indulge them-
> selves in idleness and riot. I have been told, by a consid-
> erable manufacturer, that in the year 1740, when bread
> and provisions of all kinds were very dear, his workmen
> not only made a shift to live, but paid debts, which they
> had contracted in former years, that were much more
> favourable and abundant.[25]

Hutcheson, on this occasion in agreement with his fellow
writers, said: " . . . if a people have not acquired an habit of
industry, the cheapness of all necessities of life (high 'real'
wages) rather encourages sloth," which, he said, "should be
punished by temporary servitude at least." [26]

Smith did not fully accept the views of his predecessors
about the backward sloping supply curve of labor. He al-
tered the emphasis of the doctrine by stating:

> The liberal reward of labour, as it encourages the propa-
> gation, so it increases the industry of the common people.
> The wages of labour are the encouragement of industry,
> . . . Where wages are high, accordingly, we shall always
> find the workmen more active, diligent, and expeditious,
> than where they are low . . . . Some workmen, indeed, when
> they can earn in four days what will maintain them
> through the week, will be idle the other three. *This, how-
> ever, is by no means the case with the greater part.*[27]

This was Smith's view in 1776. Thirteen years earlier his
opinion had been much more in line with David Hume's:

> Accordingly we find that in the commercial parts of Eng-
> land, the tradesmen are for the most part in a despicable
> condition; their work through half the week is sufficient
> to maintain them, and through want of education they

25. Hume, *Essays Moral, Political and Literary*, I, 357.
26. Hutcheson, *System of Moral Philosophy*, II, 318–319.
27. *The Wealth of Nations*, I, 83 (italics supplied).

have no amusement for the other, but riot and debauch-
ery. So it may very justly be said that the people who
clothe the whole world are in rags themselves.[28]

Despite this point of view, Adam Smith, at the same time
(1763), voiced his opposition to the Mandevillian thesis in
the following words:

> It is commonly imagined that whatever people spend in
> their own country cannot diminish public opulence, if
> you take care of exports and imports. This is the founda-
> tion of Dr. Mandeville's system that private vices are
> public benefits: what is spent at home is all spent among
> ourselves, none of it goes out of the country.[29]

The 1763 *Lectures* illustrate in a rudimentary fashion the
1776 Smithian thesis of the unconditional benefits flowing
from public and private parsimony. In arguing against Mandeville's thesis that domestic expenditure on luxury goods
created employment and raised the level of effective demand, Smith employed a line of reasoning which was later
developed into the implicit assumption that "saving is investing": "If I spend a thousand pounds worth of goods at
home upon myself the country is only deprived of one thousand pounds as the money still remains." [30] And again:

> It is evident that when any man tears, and wears, and
> spends his stock, without employing himself in any species
> of industry, the nation is at the end of the year so much
> the poorer by it. If he spends only the interest of the
> money he does no harm, *as the capital still remains, and
> is employed in promoting industry,* but if he spends the
> capital, the whole is gone. . . . This shows the absurdity
> of that opinion that no home consumption can hurt the
> opulence of a country.[31]

These quotations from the Smith of 1763, illustrate his
unawareness of the basic economic truth, enunciated by

28. *Lectures of Adam Smith*, p. 257.
29. *Ibid.*, pp. 207–208.
30. *Ibid.*, p. 209.
31. *Ibid.*, pp. 208–209.

many of his predecessors, that the level of effective demand could be raised through domestic expenditure on goods other than those classified as the necessities of life.

In the *Wealth of Nations* Smith developed his argument against luxury expenditure into a consistent analysis of saving and investment. In 1763 he grounded his objection to the Mandevillian thesis in the doctrine, inherited from Hutcheson, that money (income) not spent in one way will be spent in another. By 1776 he had incorporated this doctrine into the fabric of his eulogy of parsimony.

Smith's belief in the efficacy of investment in productive industries and his view that luxury expenditure dissipated economic resources is clearly seen in the following quotation:

> In mercantile and manufacturing towns, where the inferior ranks of the people are chiefly maintained by the employment of capital, they are in general, industrious, sober and thriving. . . . In those towns which are principally supported by the constant or occasional residence of a court, and in which the inferior ranks of the people are chiefly maintained by the spending of revenue, they are in general, idle, dissolute and poor.[32]

The effect of the introduction of revenue and capital into his analysis is illustrated by this extract:

> There was little trade or industry in Edinburgh before the Union. When the Scotch parliament was no longer to be assembled in it, when it ceased to be the necessary residence of the principal nobility and gentry of Scotland, it became a city of some trade and industry. It still continues, however, to be the residence of the principal courts of justice in Scotland, of the boards of customs and excise, etc. A considerable revenue, therefore, still continues to be spent in it. In trade and industry it is much inferior to Glasgow, of which the inhabitants are chiefly maintained by the employment of capital.[33]

32. *Wealth of Nations*, I, 318.
33. *Ibid.*, p. 319.

When discussing this same point in the *Lectures* he attributed idleness in Edinburgh to the lack of independence on the part of the inhabitants:

> In Glasgow, where almost nobody has more than one servant, there are fewer capital crimes than in Edinburgh. . . . Upon this principle, therefore, it is not so much the police that prevents the commission of crimes as the having of as few persons as possible to live upon others. Nothing tends so much to corrupt mankind as dependency, while independency still increases the honesty of the people. The establishment of commerce and manufactures, which brings about this independency, is the best police for preventing crimes.[34]

The following quotations demonstrate Smith's analysis of saving and investment.

> The proportion between capital and revenue, therefore, seems everywhere to regulate the proportion between industry and idleness. Where ever capital predominates, industry prevails: wherever revenue, idleness.[35]

Having got this far, Smith concluded that "Capitals are increased by parsimony, and diminished by prodigality and misconduct." [36]

He implicitly assumed that all capital was or would be invested. On the basis of this assumption he argued that national productive capacity would be increased only if capital was accumulated:

> Every increase or diminution of capital, therefore, naturally tends to increase or diminish the real quantity of industry, the number of productive hands, and consequently the exchangeable value of the annual produce of the land and labour of the country, the real wealth and revenue of all its inhabitants.[37]

---

34. *Lectures of Adam Smith*, p. 155.
35. *Wealth of Nations*, I, 319–320.
36. *Ibid.*, p. 320.
37. *Ibid.*, p. 320.

The *non-sequitur* displayed here can be traced back to Hutcheson's seemingly innocuous words that "the money saved to the housekeeper would afford either better dress, or other conveniences to a family, which would equally support artificiers." [38] Accepting this statement, Smith concluded that all revenue over and above the amount needed to maintain life's necessities would be more advantageously employed in the form of saving, which is the *same* as investment. As more revenue became invested by the act of saving, so more people would become employed. He thought the doctrine that the expenditure of income on luxury goods to increase employment was a foolish one, and he dismissed it out of hand. He believed that this kind of action would create idleness: in his view, only capital (saving automatically invested) could create desirable habits of industry and lead to an upsurge in national prosperity. Thus, the constant aim of the community should be to amass as much capital as possible.

> Whatever a person saves from his revenue he adds to his capital, and either employs it himself in maintaining an additional number of productive hands, or enables some other person to do so, by lending it to him for an interest, that is, for a share of profits. As the capital of an individual can be increased only by what he saves from his annual revenue or his annual gains, so the capital of a society, which is the same with that of all the individuals who compose it, can be increased only in the same manner.[39]

Smith does not even link the cause of prosperity with production. He unconditionally praised the positive act of parsimony as the fountain from which all economic prosperity flowed.

> Parsimony, and not industry, is the immediate cause of the increase of capital. Industry, indeed, provides the subject

38. Hutcheson, *Reflections upon Laughter*, pp. 64–65.
39. *Wealth of Nations*, I, 320.

which parsimony accumulates. But whatever industry might acquire, if *parsimony did not save and store up*, the capital would never be the greater.[40]

Smith's fulsome praise of parsimony not only identified saving with investment, but attributed to the mere act of saving the economic function of increasing the national product. Drawing on his concept of the labor theory of value, he continued:

Parsimony, by increasing the fund [capital] which is destined for the maintenance of productive hands, tends to increase the number of those hands whose labour adds to the value of the subject upon which it is bestowed. It tends therefore to increase the exchangeable value of the annual produce of the land and labour of the country. It puts into motion an additional quantity of industry, which gives an additional value to the annual produce.[41]

Smith believed that parsimony alone, without assistance from luxury consumption, increased total national production. He implicitly assumed that aggregate demand and aggregate supply tended to be automatically self-adjusting and self-equilibrating at an optimum level. Therefore, because parsimony "raised up new hands," it not only boosted production to new levels, but also raised the level of demand without resorting to the morally degrading and economically wasteful act of the dissipation of revenue by the encouragement of luxury expenditure. His unqualified praise of parsimony is complete: "every prodigal appears to be a public enemy and every frugal man a public benefactor." [42] So deeply ingrained in man's character was "the desire of bettering our condition," and because the "passion for present enjoyment" is in general only momentary and occasional, "the principle of frugality seems not only to predominate, but to predominate very greatly." [43]

40. *Ibid.* (italics supplied).
41. *Ibid.*, p. 320.
42. *Ibid.*, p. 323.
43. *Ibid.*, pp. 322–323.

Smith's eulogy of parsimony, his doctrine that saving *is* investment, had serious results in several lines of economic inquiry. In this respect Hutcheson's influence on his thought was detrimental. If Smith had followed the urbane and sensible Hume, the long and weary struggle which Keynes and his successors fought for the rediscovery of the economic truth that the chief aggregates of macroeconomic analysis are not elegantly self-regulating, might well have been unnecessary.

CHAPTER V

TRADE: INTERNATIONAL
AND DOMESTIC

Although Hutcheson was not a forceful advocate of regulated, state-managed international trade policies, he nevertheless tended to support such contemporary doctrines. The key to these doctrines is to be found in the then generally accepted contemporary concept of national wealth. Economic policy in Hutcheson's day was governed by the conception of national wealth as being a stock for goods useful to the nation for the furthering and achievement of nationalistic aims. Hutcheson believed that industry is the natural mine of wealth, the fund for all stores for exportation, by the surplus of which, beyond the value of what a nation imports, it must increase in wealth and power.[1]

This point of view was more or less typical of contemporary economic reasoning. An excess of exports over imports, the favorable balance-of-trade theory, was the ultimate aim of most trade policy designed to enrich the nation. In general, Hutcheson supported those doctrines which advocated the achievement of as favorable a balance of trade as possible. It would be unjustified, however, to describe him as an outright proponent of this policy.

Hutcheson listed the various measures which he thought should be undertaken to achieve the desired national trading surplus of exports over imports:

1. *System of Moral Philosophy*, II, 318.

Diligent agriculture must furnish the necessaries of life, and the materials for all manufactures: and all mechanick arts should be encouraged to prepare them for use and exportation. Goods prepared for export should generally be free from all burdens and taxes, and so should the goods be which are necessarily consumed by the artificers, as much as possible; that no other country be able to undersell like goods at a foreign market. Where one country alone has certain materials they may safely impose duties upon them when exported; but such moderate ones as shall not prevent the consumption of them abroad.[2]

In this respect, Hutcheson was a creature of his time. He thought trade policy should encourage, by legislation, the largest possible surplus of exports in order to achieve the commonly accepted end of national supremacy.

Believing, as he did, that the only firm foundation for such a trade policy was national industry, he waxed eloquent about the dangers of sloth. "If a people have not acquired an habit of industry, the cheapness of all the necessaries of life, rather encourages sloth."[3] To insure that the desired habit of industry was inculcated in the nation, he believed that "the best remedy is to raise the demand for all necessaries; not merely by premiums upon exporting them, which is often useful too; but by increasing the number of people, who consume them."[4] To help bring about this eminently satisfactory state of affairs:

Industrious foreigners should therefore be invited to us, and all men of industry should live with us unmolested and easy. Encouragement should be given to marriage and to those who rear a numerous offspring to industry. The unmarried should pay higher taxes, as they are not at the charge of rearing new subjects to the state. Any foolish notions of meanness in mechanick arts, as if they were unworthy of men of better families, should be borne

2. *Ibid.*
3. *Ibid.*
4. *Ibid.*, pp. 318–319.

down, and men of better conditions as to birth, or fortune engaged to be concerned in such occupations.[5]

Hutcheson's work, however, is notable for the manner in which it refines and improves certain of the cruder ideas about state-regulated trade policies. One of these refinements was concerned with the importation of goods for their eventual re-export to more favorable markets. This was one of the earlier theoretical enunciations of the trade policy which eventually culminated in the establishment of England as a great entrepôt country.

> Foreign materials should be imported and even premiums given, when necessary, that all our hands may be employed; and that, by exporting them again manufactured, we may obtain from abroad the price of our labours.[6]

This prescription did not complete Hutcheson's remedy for creating a favorable balance of trade, for he also advocated that the home consumption of manufactured imports should be damped down by the imposition of a set of high import duties.

> Foreign manufactures and products ready for consumption, should be made dear to the consumer by high duties, if we cannot altogether prohibit the consumption; that they may never be used by the lower and more numerous orders of the people, whose consumption would be far greater than those of the few who are wealthy.[7]

This strand of nationalistic thought was reflected, too, in Hutcheson's views on navigation and sea transport. In modern terms, he maintained that since earnings from shipping would help to swell both the visible and invisible export accounts, this branch of transport should be given every legislative encouragement:

> Navigation, or the carriage of goods foreign and domestick, should be encouraged, as a gainful branch of busi-

5. *Ibid.*, p. 319.
6. *Ibid.*
7. *Ibid.*

ness, surpassing often all the profit made by the merchant. This too is a nursery of fit hands for defence at sea.[8]

In the *Introduction to Moral Philosophy* Hutcheson, as is usual in this book, made the same points with greater clarity of thought and economy of expression.

And in like manner all mechanick arts, either simpler, or more elegant, should be encouraged, lest our wealth be drained by our buying foreign manufactures. Merchandize and fishery are of great consequence. Nay the very building of ships too, that we may not lose the profit of the carriage either of our own or foreign goods, and with this, the training of sailors; which contributes both to the increase of wealth and to the defence of the state in war. The mechanick trades should be held in reputation, so that people of better fortunes and families may not deem it below them to be concerned in them.[9]

The conclusion is clear. Hutcheson believed in the efficiency of governmental control and intervention in order to achieve national supremacy, and he advocated various policy measures designed to increase the value of exports over the value of imports. It would be grossly unfair, however, to classify him as an ardent supporter of trade-control policies, since he also put forward much more liberal trade policies than many of those proposed by his predecessors and contemporaries.

After David Hume and Adam Smith had published their works, "mercantilism," as Smith designated that large, heterogeneous mass of economic literature which in one way or another advocated the regulation of national trade policies, was largely rejected by succeeding prominent British commentators. One of the main factors leading to the collapse of this kind of economic philosophy was the formulation of what Jacob Viner called "the theory of the self regulating

8. *Ibid.*, pp. 319–320.
9. *Introduction to Moral Philosophy*, pp. 308–309.

mechanism of international specie distribution." [10] The first pronounced and full statement of this theory in Britain before the nineteenth century was made by David Hume. While various elements of the theory had been stated before his influential exposition, Hume succeeded in combining the various strands into an integrated analysis.

The formulation of the theory was probably the first effective onslaught on so-called "mercantilist" international trade policy. Hume demonstrated lucidly that it was unnecessary to promote the internal accumulation of specie by a favorable balance of trade. He maintained that this kind of action contained the seeds of self-destruction. In the absence of government intervention, a country with a scarce metallic currency would find that the prices of goods would fall. Hence, for other countries, it would be cheaper to buy these lower priced commodities; thus the country's exports would rise and the balance of trade would become favorable; an inflow of specie would be attracted from abroad. Conversely, should money become plentiful in a country, domestic prices would rise relatively to those or other countries; its exports would consequently fall and an unfavorable balance of trade would be established which would have to be balanced by a draining off of specie.

Hume stated this theory with a degree of clarity, completeness of exposition, and emphasis on its importance far superior to any analysis attempted by his predecessors.[11] Hume's reason for developing his self-equilibrating theory was to show that the national supply of money would automatically regulate itself without the need for governmental intervention. The dominant role was played by changes in price levels which brought about adjustments of the trade

10. *Studies in the Theory of International Trade* (New York: Harper and Brothers, 1937), p. 74.
11. Hume had stated his theory of the self-regulating mechanism of international specie distribution as early as 1749. See his letter to Montesquieu of April 10, 1749, and to James Oswald of Dunnikier, Nov. 1, 1750, in *Letters of David Hume*, I, 133–138 and 142–144.

balances, assisted to a minor degree by fluctuations in exchange rates.[12]

He begins his discussion of the theory by assuming that four-fifths of all the money in Britain has been destroyed overnight, and then proceeds to trace the consequences flowing from this assumption.

> Suppose four-fifths of all the money in Great Britain to be annihilated in one night, and the nation reduced to the same condition, with regard to specie, as in the reigns of the Harrys and Edwards, what would be the consequence? Must not the price of all labour and commodities sink in proportion, and everything be sold as cheap as they were in those ages? What nation could then dispute with us in any foreign market, or pretend to navigate or to sell manufactures at the same price, which to us would afford sufficient profit? In how little time, therefore, must this bring back the money which we had lost, and raise us to the level of all the neighbouring nations? Where, after we have arrived, we immediately lose the advantage of the cheapness of labour and commodities; and the farther flowing in of money is stopped by our fulness and repletion.[13]

His next hypothesis assumed that the money supply in Great Britain was multiplied fivefold overnight.

> Again, suppose, that all the money in Great Britain were multiplied fivefold in a night, must not the contrary effect follow? Must not all labour and commodities rise to such an exorbitant height, that no neighbouring nations could afford to buy from us; while their commodities, on the other hand, became comparatively so cheap, that, in spite of all the laws that could be formed, they would be run in upon us, and our money flow out; till we fall to a level with foreigners, and lose that great superiority of riches, which had laid us under such disadvantages? [14]

12. As far as I have been able to establish, Hume made this point for the first time in economic literature.
13. *Essays Moral, Political and Literary*, I, 333.
14. *Ibid.*

Hume held that the same causes which produced this self-regulating mechanism under "miraculous" conditions, must also prevent any great inequality occurring under normal trading conditions.

> Now, it is evident, that the same causes, which could correct these exorbitant inequalities, were they to happen miraculously, must prevent their happening in the common course of nature, and must for ever, in all neighbouring nations, preserve money nearly proportionable to the art and industry of each nation.[15]

He did not apply his theory to international trade matters only. He considered that the mechanism operated internally between different districts of a single country, and preserved an approximately equal level between the different provinces.

> How is the balance kept in the provinces of every kingdom among themselves, but by the force of this principle, which makes it impossible for money to lose its level, and either to rise or sink beyond the proportion of the labour and commodities which are in each province.[16]

As an additional equilibrating factor he included the influence of variations in the exchange rate. This was a minor factor operating to correct an adverse balance of trade, for if the trade balance was unfavorable, the exchanges would move against England, acting as a new stimulus to exports.

> There is another cause, though more limited in its operation, which checks the wrong balance of trade, to every particular nation to which the kingdom trades. When we import more goods than we export, the exchange turns against us, and this becomes a new encouragement to export; as much as the charge of carriage and insurance of the money which becomes due would amount to. For the exchange would never rise but a little higher than that sum.[17]

15. *Ibid.*
16. *Ibid.*, pp. 334–335.
17. *Ibid.*, p. 333.

In conclusion, Hume outlined the stimulus which kept the whole mechanism in operation.

> We need not have recourse to a physical attraction, in order to explain the necessity of this operation. There is a moral attraction, arising from the interests and passions of men, which is full as potent and infallible.[18]

Thus, the profit motive, acting under the stimulus of price differentials gently but irrevocably controlled the operation.

Hume held that international trade mechanism operated to bring money to a common level in all countries just as "all water, wherever it communicates remains always at a level." [19] By the level of money he understood the proportion between money and commodities.

> It must carefully be remarked, that throughout this discourse, wherever I speak of the level of money, I mean always its proportional level to the commodities, labour, industry and skill, which is in the several states. And I assert, that where these advantages are double, triple, quadruple to what these are in the neighbouring states, the money infallibility will also be double, triple, quadruple. The only circumstance that can obstruct the exactness of these proportions, is the expence of transporting the commodities from one place to another; and this expence is sometimes unequal. Thus the corn, cattle, cheese, butter, of Derbyshire cannot draw the money of London, so much as the manufacturers of London, draw the money of Derbyshire. But this objection is only a seeming one: For so far as the transport of commodities is expensive, so far is the communication between the places obstructed and imperfect.[20]

With regard to the advisability of a nation participating in international trade, Hume's position was clear. He held that international trade increased the power of the state and, at the same time, promoted the happiness of the people.

18. *Ibid.*, p. 334.
19. *Ibid.*, p. 333.
20. *Ibid.*, pp. 335–336.

> The same method of reasoning will let us see the advantage of *foreign* commerce, in augmenting the power of the state, as well as the riches and happiness of the people. It increases the stock of labour in the nation. . . . by its imports, furnishes materials for new manufactures; and by its exports, it produces labour in particular commodities, which could not be consumed at home. In short, a kingdom, that has a large import and export, must abound more with industry, and that upon delicacies and luxuries, than a kingdom, which rests contented with its native commodities. It is, therefore, more powerful, as well as richer and happier.[21]

And again:

> It is very usual, in nations ignorant of the nature of commerce, to prohibit the exportations of commodities, and to preserve among themselves whatever they think valuable and useful. They do not consider that, in this prohibition, they act directly contrary to their intention, and that the more is exported of any commodity, the more will be raised at home.[22]

To attempt to create a favorable trade balance by restraints upon imports and exports was, he thought, futile policy.

In effect, Hume pointed to the natural foundation of commerce in the international division of labor, and he showed that one nation's prosperity was a help to the prosperity of its neighbors, and not a hindrance.

> Nothing is more usual, among states which have made some advances in commerce, than to look on the progress of their neighbours with a suspicious eye, to consider all trading states as their rivals, and to suppose that it is impossible for any one of them to flourish, but at their expence. In opposition to this narrow and malignant opinion, I will venture to assert, that the encrease of riches and commerce in any one nation, instead of hurting, commonly promotes the riches and commerce of all its neighbours . . . . where an open communication is preserved

21. *Ibid.*, p. 295.
22. *Ibid.*, p. 331.

among nations, it is impossible but the domestic industry of every one must receive an encrease from the improvements of the others.[23]

He completely departed from the narrow nationalistic point of view of his predecessors, as the following passage so vividly shows.

I shall therefore venture to acknowledge, that, not only as a man, but as a British subject, I pray for the flourishing commerce of Germany, Spain, Italy, and even France itself. I am at least certain, that Great Britain, and all those nations, would flourish more, did their sovereigns and ministers adopt such enlarged and benevolent sentiments towards each other.[24]

To help achieve this end, he condemned

those numberless bars, obstructions, and imposts, which all nations of Europe, and none more than England, have put upon trade; from an exorbitant desire of amassing money, which never will heap up beyond its level, while it circulates; or from an ill-grounded apprehension of losing their specie, which never will sink below it. Could anything scatter our riches, it would be such impolitic contrivances.[25]

Although Hume supplied the ammunition which eventually led to the rejection of ultra-nationalistic trade policies, it must be borne in mind that he was not a complete free trader. On the question of the protection of infant industries he retained an interventionist point of view. He approved for example, of taxes on German linen and French brandy.

All taxes, however, upon foreign commodities, are not to be regarded as prejudicial or useless, but those only which are founded on the jealousy above-mentioned. A tax on German linen encourages home manufactures, and thereby multiplies our people and industry. Taxes on brandy increase the sale of rum, and support our southern colonies.[26]

23. *Ibid.*, p. 345.
24. *Ibid.*, p. 348.
25. *Ibid.*, p. 343.
26. *Ibid.*, pp. 343-344.

Thus, there is an inherent contradiction in his work. While he advocated freer trade, he also retained faint traces of what may be called a refined restrictionism. His work bridged the transitional period from the old to the new views, while his criticism of the desirability of treasure marked the zenith of informed thought on this subject. His unique contribution to the theory of international and domestic trade lies in his lucid exposition of the self-regulating mechanism, which lifts the quality of his work far above that of his predecessors, and, it might be said, far above that of most of his immediate successors.[27]

Adam Smith devoted Book IV of the *Wealth of Nations*, entitled "Of Systems of Political Oeconomy," to an elaborate propagandist polemic against the "Mercantile System." In English economic literature prior to Adam Smith and David Hume, "mercantilism," defined in Smithian terms, is easily the most pervasive doctrine. It was Smith himself who gave the name "commercial" or "mercantile," to the system which eventually became known as "mercantilism."

Smith led up to his statement of international trade theory from the benefits of the division of labor. In proceeding in this way, Smith was merely following an outline previously mapped out by, among others, Charles Davenant, Isaac Gervaise, and Patrick Lindsay.[28] Nevertheless, there is little evidence to show that these and other earlier writers were influential on Smith, or for that matter, on Hume. It has already been noted how Hume, while disparaging in a most urbane manner the monetary and balance-of-trade doctrines of the time, still retained some elements of protection in his analysis. Similarly, Adam Smith both in the *Lectures* and in

27. Viner, *op. cit.*, p. 74, states that in "Richard Cantillon's *Essai sur la nature du commerce en général* the self-regulating mechanism is clearly and ably expounded," but "I have found no evidence that any part of his exposition of the self-regulating mechanism appeared in print before 1752, or that Hume was influenced, directly or indirectly, by Cantillon."
28. See Viner, *op. cit.*, pp. 103–110.

the *Wealth of Nations* relapsed at times into varying versions of the same doctrine.

> If I purchase a thousand pounds' worth of French wines, and drink them all when they come home, the country is two thousand pounds poorer, because both the goods and the money are gone; if I spend a thousand pounds worth of goods at home upon myself the country is only deprived of one thousand pounds, as the money still remains; but in maintaining an army in a distant war, it is the same thing whether we pay them in goods or money, because the consumption is the same at any rate.[29]

Although Smith's teaching on the matter of free trade was not altogether unqualified, it was on the whole, where questions of exchanges of every kind are concerned, very much in favor of complete freedom. He began his discussion as follows:

> It is the maxim of every prudent master of a family, never to attempt to make at home what it will cost him more to make than to buy. The taylor does not attempt to make his own shoes, but buys them of the shoemaker. . . . What is prudence in the conduct of every private family, can scarce be folly in that of a great kingdom. If a foreign country can supply us with a commodity cheaper than we ourselves can make it, better buy it of them with some part of the produce of our own industry, employed in a way in which we have some advantage.[30]

Smith firmly believed that in the actual conditions of trade, the economic advantages flowing from a policy of free trade had been overlooked. In fact, he said that the British Empire had been organized along "mercantilist" lines.

> A great empire has been established for the sole purpose of raising up a nation of customers who should be obliged to buy from the shops of our different producers, all the goods with which these could supply them. . . . It cannot

29. *Lectures of Adam Smith*, p. 209.
30. *Wealth of Nations*, I, 422.

be very difficult to determine who have been the contrivers of this whole mercantile system; not the consumers, we may believe, whose interest has been entirely neglected; but the producers, whose interest has been so carefully attended to; and among the latter class our merchants and manufacturers have been by far the principal architects.[31]

Smith was cognizant of political as well as economic interests. He was therefore prepared to grant that an industry essential for defense purposes should be protected on the grounds "that defence is of much more importance than opulence," and he pronounced the Navigation Act to have been "perhaps the wisest of all the commercial regulations of England." He also thought that when a tax was imposed on home production, a similar tax should be imposed on competing foreign imports. While propounding a firm free-trade theory, Smith did not believe that his advocacy would be successful.

To expect, indeed, that the freedom of trade should ever be entirely restored in Great Britain, is as absurd as to expect that an Oceana or Utopia should ever be established in it. Not only the prejudices of the public, but what is much more unconquerable, the private interests of many individuals, irresistibly oppose it.[32]

Government was so intimidated by the large monopolies which had stimulated the protectionist policies that it was no longer strong enough to oppose them.

This monopoly has so much increased the number of some particular tribes of them, [manufacturers] that, like an overgrown standing army, they have become formidable to the government, and upon many occasions intimidate the legislature.[33]

Despite the various qualifications raised by both Smith and Hume in their critiques of "mercantilist" thinking, the

31. *Ibid.*, II, 160.
32. *Ibid.*, I, 435.
33. *Ibid.*, pp. 435–436.

period following the publication of their works witnessed the steady erosion of the "Mercantile System." This result, however, was due mainly to the force and brilliance of the theoretical expositions of Hume and Smith.

Although Adam Smith was intimately acquainted with Hume and his works, he made no reference at all in the *Wealth of Nations* to the self-regulating mechanism in terms of price levels and trade balances.[34] Smith was content to confine his theory of international specie distribution to the obsolete terms of the amount of money, unrelated to the relative price level, required by each country to circulate its trade. When a country has a surplus of money for this purpose, the excess money will be sent abroad, "to seek that profitable employment which it cannot find at home." [35]

> Let us suppose, for example, that the whole circulating money of some particular country amounted, at a particular time, to one million sterling, that sum being then sufficient for circulating the whole annual produce of their land and labour. Let us suppose too, that sometime thereafter, different banks and bankers issued promissory notes, payable to the bearer, to the extent of one million, reserving in their different coffers two hundred thousand pounds for answering occasional demands. There would remain, therefore, in circulation, eight hundred thousand pounds in gold and silver, and a million of bank notes, or eighteen hundred thousand pounds of paper and money together. But the annual produce of the land and labour of country had before required only one million to circulate and distribute it to its proper consumers, and that annual produce cannot be immediately augmented by those operations of banking. . . . The channel of circulation, if I may be allowed such an expression, will remain precisely the same as before. One million we have supposed sufficient to fill that channel. Whatever, therefore, is poured into it beyond this sum, cannot run in it, but must overflow. One million eight

---

34. Viner, *op. cit.*, p. 87.
35. *Wealth of Nations*, I, 277.

hundred thousand pounds are poured into it. Eight hundred thousand pounds, therefore, must overflow, that sum being over and above what can be employed in the circulation of the country. But though this sum cannot be employed at home, it is too valuable to be allowed to lie idle. It will, therefore, be sent abroad, in order to seek that profitable employment which it cannot find at home.[36]

This is a very different and inferior exposition of the self-regulating mechanism put forward by his friend, David Hume. The mystery which surrounds the reasons why Smith decided not to incorporate Hume's self-regulating mechanism into his own analysis grows greater when it is seen that the *Lectures* approvingly summarize Hume's analysis.

Mr. Hume published some essays showing the absurdity of these and other such doctrines. He proves very ingeniously that money must always bear a certain proportion to the quantity of commodities in every country; that whenever money is accumulated beyond the proportion of commodities in any country, the price of goods will necessarily rise; that this country will be undersold at the foreign markets, and consequently the money must depart, into other nations; but on the contrary whenever the quantity of money falls below the proportion of goods, the price of goods diminishes, the country undersells others in foreign markets, and consequently money returns in great plenty. Thus money and goods will keep near about a certain level in every country. Mr. Hume's reasoning is exceedingly ingenious.[37]

Thus, Hume's analysis of the self-adjusting mechanism of monetary flows was at first, in Smith's initial thinking, approvingly adopted and taught. Later on, however, motivated by some inexplicable reason, he omitted Hume's lucid observations from his account of trade theory and practice.

It is extremely difficult to decide just how strong an influence was exerted on Adam Smith by David Hume's perspicuous reasonings on international trade. Undoubtedly,

36. *Ibid.*
37. *Lectures*, p. 197.

both Hume and Smith must be considered as the main architects of the eventual downfall of the "mercantilist" doctrines, for after they had written, the doctrines were forced on to the defensive. Neither were complete free traders, but neither accepted the cruder versions of contemporary trade policies.

While Smith followed Hume's general reasoning on international trade, he did not accept, or make use of, all Hume's most valuable contributions to the theory. While leaning heavily on Hume, Smith did not accept Hume's central and most brilliant argument against the balance-of-trade doctrines. It seems likely that Smith's chief indebtedness in this field was more to the philosophers than to the earlier political economists. For this reason it is probably true that "Hume the philosopher," rather than "Hume the economist," exerted the greater influence on Smith. In the same manner, it was probably "Hutcheson the philosopher" and not "Hutcheson the economist" of the relatively few, scattered, but acute, economic remarks, who contributed most to the formulation of Adam Smith's free-trade policy.

CHAPTER VI

MAXIMS OF TAXATION

Hutcheson's remarks on this subject are concise and forward-looking. His condensed, compact sentences are probably the source of most of Adam Smith's celebrated maxims of taxation.

Smith's first and fourth maxims are clearly stated in Hutcheson's opening remarks.

> As to taxes for defraying the publick expenses, those are most convenient which are laid on matters of luxury and splendour, rather than the necessaries of life; on foreign products and manufactures, rather than domestick; and such as can be easily raised without many expensive offices for collecting them. But above all, a just proportion to the wealth of the people should be observed in whatever is raised from them, otherways than by duties upon foreign products and manufactures, for such duties are often necessary to encourage industry at home, tho' there were no publick expenses.[1]

This quotation indicates that Smith's first maxim, equality of taxation, had received special emphasis by Hutcheson: "But above all, a just proportion to the wealth of the people should be observed in whatever is raised from them."

When Smith turned to this maxim he expressed the same idea in words similar to those used by Hutcheson.

> "The expence of government to the individuals of a great nation, is like the expence of management to the joint

1. Hutcheson, *System of Moral Philosophy*, II, 340–341.

tenants of a great estate, who are all obliged to contribute in proportion to their respective interests in the estate. In the observation or neglect of this maxim consists, what is called the equality or inequality of taxation." [2]

Adam Smith's second maxim of taxation, however, the certainty of taxation, was not mentioned by Hutcheson, even in the briefest manner.

Hutcheson's contention that "those [taxes] are most convenient which are laid on matters of luxury and splendour, rather than the necessaries of life; on foreign products and manufactures, rather than domestick" can be considered to be the embryonic form of Smith's third maxim, convenience of payment. It seems highly likely that Smith expanded this brief Hutchesonian suggestion of the third maxim into his more detailed treatment, as expressed in this extract.

"Every tax ought to be levied at the time, or in the manner, in which it is most likely to be convenient for the contributor to pay it. . . . Taxes upon such consumable goods as are articles of luxury, are all finally paid by the consumer, and generally in a manner that is very convenient for him." [3]

Adam Smith's fourth maxim is economy in collection. Here again, it is not difficult to find in Hutcheson's work hints of Smith's subsequent treatment: "and such as can be easily raised without many expensive offices for collecting them." [4] Adam Smith extended these few but suggestive words into a much longer explanation of how economy in collection can be achieved and why it is a desirable element in a taxation system. Smith's first sentence in his section dealing with this fourth maxim, states his purpose: "Every tax ought to be so contrived as both to take out and to keep out of the pockets of the people as little as possible, over and above what it brings into the public treasury of the state." [5]

2. *Wealth of Nations*, II, 310.
3. *Wealth of Nations*, II, 311.
4. *System*, II, 341.
5. *Wealth of Nations*, II, 311.

Hutcheson's aim in discussing taxation was to emphasize that equality of taxation should be observed, so far as possible. Hutcheson realized that complete equality could not be achieved unless government was able, at regular intervals of every five, six, or seven years, to obtain a detailed record of all the wealth of the families in the nation. In other words, he wanted a regular census instituted. "This proportion can never be observed without a *census* or an estimation made of all the wealth of private families at frequently recurring periods." [6] He thought that such a census would fulfill two valuable tasks in that it would "detect perhaps a few broken merchants and men of business, and both turn them out of trade and prevent their opportunities of defrauding more creditors." [7] But much more important and more relevant to the topic under discussion, "By a *census* all would be burdened proportionally to their wealth; and thus the publick expences be oppressive to none beyond his neighbours." [8]

Thus, according to Hutcheson, a census would serve as a basis on which to erect a system of proportionate taxation and pave the way for the equality of taxation which he rated so highly. His appeal for the aid of 'political arithmetic' would have delighted the heart of Sir William Petty. It was Hutcheson's firm belief that there was "no other possible method, of making men contribute in just proportions to the publick charge, than by instituting a *census*, or valuation of all their fortunes." [9]

After this point had been so emphatically elaborated it is surprising that Adam Smith completely ignored it. While Smith made equality of taxation his first maxim, he did not advocate the institution of a national census as an aid towards achieving his end. Perhaps it was his distrust of 'polit-

6. *System*, II, 341.
7. *Ibid.*
8. *Ibid.*
9. *Introduction to Moral Philosophy*, p. 325.

ical arithmetic' that led him to overlook the good sense of Hutcheson's advocacy of a census. Certainly, he was aware of the existence of this procedure, for he acknowledged Gregory King's skill with statistics,[10] but he expressed his lack of faith in the subject by saying, "I have no great faith in political arithmetic, and I mean not to warrant the exactness of either of these computations." [11] From this point of view, Hutcheson's faith in statistics has been justified by subsequent developments, while Smith's caution has proved to be without foundation.

Hume's remarks on taxation are much more detailed than those of Hutcheson. Hume opened his discussion by criticizing the commonly held belief "that every new tax creates a new ability in the subject to bear it, and that each encrease of public burdens encreases proportionably the industry of the people." [12]

Hume granted that this maxim had some foundation both in reason and experience, but looked on it with a suspicious eye, for he was well aware that it was open to abuse by unscrupulous governments. He pointed out that a tax imposed upon necessities results in any one of three consequences. Either the poor must lower their standard of living, or their wages must be raised, or they must work harder to increase their productivity (without pressing for higher wages) in order to maintain their pretax standard of living. He believed that this last alternative naturally followed when taxes were moderate and not imposed on the necessities of life. Hence he assumed that this result was a good end in itself, for it stimulated the increased production of national output.

> Where taxes are moderate, are laid on gradually, and affect not the necessaries of life, this consequence naturally follows; and it is certain, that such difficulties often serve

10. *Wealth of Nations*, I, 79.
11. *Ibid.*, II, 36.
12. *Essays Moral, Political and Literary*, I, 356.

to excite the industry of a people, and render them more opulent and laborious, than others, who enjoy the greatest advantages.[13]

This quotation is perhaps more notable for supplementing Hutcheson's dictum that, "those taxes are most convenient which are laid on matters of luxury and splendour rather than the necessaries of life," [14] which foreshadowed Smith's third maxim—convenience of payment—than for its contextual significance. While still dealing with the maxim "that every new tax creates a new ability in the subject to bear it," Hume uttered a warning that the maxim must not be abused, since unduly harsh taxes ultimately destroy the incentive to work and produce. Even before this undesirable end is reached, the imposition of harsh taxes certainly forces up wages and the prices of all goods, and so leads to a reduction in real income.

Hume was quite definite in his statement about what he considered to be the best kinds of taxes.

> The best taxes are such as are levied upon consumptions, especially those of luxury; because such taxes are least felt by the people. They seem, in some measure, voluntary; since a man may chuse how far he will use the commodity which is taxed. They are paid gradually and insensibly: they naturally produce sobriety and frugality, if judiciously imposed: And being confounded with the natural price of the commodity, they are scarcely perceived by the consumers.[15]

This is another anticipation of Adam Smith's third maxim—convenience of payment.

Like Hutcheson, Hume advocated economy in the collection of taxes. Admittedly, he had little to say under this heading, but his few words indicated that he was at least cognizant of the importance of the notion which Smith con-

13. *Ibid.*, p. 356.
14. *System*, p. 340.
15. *Essays Moral, Political and Literary*, I, 358.

verted into his fourth maxim—economy in collection: "Taxes upon possessions are levied without expence; but have every other disadvantage." [16] Furthermore, when discussing taxes levied upon luxury consumptions, Hume stated that "their only disadvantage is, that they are expensive in the levying." [17]

Equality of taxation, or rather, the idea of proportionate taxation, for which Hutcheson had pleaded so urgently, was also urged by Hume. When condemning arbitrary taxes as being the most pernicious of all taxes, he said that "by their unfavorable inequality, they are more grievous, than by the real burden, which they impose." [18] Thus, a trace of Smith's first maxim can also be discerned in Hume's taxation analysis. From his dislike of arbitrary taxes, it can be legitimately assumed that Hume favored taxes which are certain in their incidence. "But the most pernicious of all taxes are those which are arbitrary." [19] In discussing his second maxim—certainty—Smith made the same point, and it is worth noting that this is the only one of Smith's four maxims that Hutcheson's succinct remarks do not anticipate. "The tax which each individual is bound to pay ought to be certain, and not arbitrary." [20]

To sum up, then, it will be seen that Hume, unlike Hutcheson (who foreshadowed only three of Smith's maxims), had all four maxims clearly stated in the brief compass of a few pages of his discussion. In neither Hume's nor Hutcheson's treatment were the details and expositions discussed with the refinement and clearness of Smith's, but the fact remains that Smith's maxims have their genesis in the work of these men, writing a quarter of a century or more before he published his *magnum opus*.

16. *Ibid.*
17. *Ibid.*
18. *Ibid.*
19. *Ibid.*
20. *Wealth of Nations*, II, 310.

The incidence of taxation was a topic which also captured Hume's attention. He did not agree with the then prevalent generalization "that all taxes, however levied, fall upon the land at last." [21] With rather a cynical touch, he admitted that in a Britain governed by the landed class, such an opinion fulfilled a useful purpose in that it restrained the government from imposing too many taxes on industry and trade, for the fear that land would ultimately bear the brunt of them.

In the *Wealth of Nations* there is a lengthy section dealing with taxes. From the point of view of the subsequent development of public finance, the first three pages of the eighty-one-page-long section are the most important; these three pages constitute Smith's introduction to his detailed, historical section.[22] They embody his analysis of the four maxims of taxation, equality, certainty, convenience of payment, and economy in collection. It has already been noted how the germ of each maxim is to be found in the seminal writings of Hume and Hutcheson. Needless to say, Smith's treatment of each maxim, his fine exposition of each as a formal framework, consciously stated and used as criteria by which actual taxes may be judged, is a vast improvement on the almost incidental remarks of Hutcheson and Hume. Nevertheless, his great teacher Francis Hutcheson and his intimate friend David Hume had previously pointed to their significance for taxation policy. It was left for Smith to gather them together and express them concisely as the fundamentals of taxation principles.

The remaining seventy-odd pages which Smith devoted to the examination of particular kinds of taxes need not concern us here. It is sufficient to observe that he examined against the criteria of his maxims

21. *Essays Moral, Political and Literary*, II, 359.
22. *Wealth of Nations*, II, 310–312.

those taxes which, it is intended, should fall upon rent; secondly, of those which, it is intended, should fall upon profit; thirdly, of those which, it is intended should fall upon wages; and fourthly, of those which, it is intended should fall indifferently upon all those three different sources of private revenue.[23]

Neither Hume's nor Hutcheson's work is comparable with this facet of Smith's exposition; on the other hand, neither set out to discuss the objects which Smith had in view when he developed this particular piece of analysis.

23. *Ibid.*, II, 310.

CHAPTER VII

THE THEORY OF PROPERTY

Francis Hutcheson grounded the right of property in the general sympathy of mankind, and ascribed the origin of property to public and private benevolence. He maintained that property encouraged industry, and so added to the sum total of human happiness.

> Each man has not only the selfish desires toward his own happiness and the means of it, but some tender generous affections in the several relations of life. We are all conscious of some such dispositions in ourselves, and justly conclude that others have the like. We know that these are the ordinary springs of the activity of mankind in employing their labour to cultivate the earth, or procure things useful in human life. . . . From these strong feelings in our hearts we discover the right of property that each one has in the fruits of his own labour; that is, we must approve the securing them to him, where no publick interest requires the contrary.[1]

He regarded this generous sentiment as being inherent in every human breast.

Proceeding from a consideration of the individual, he applied his theory of the "requirements of the common interest of society."

> Universal industry is plainly necessary for the support of mankind. . . . Whatever institution therefore shall be found necessary to promote universal diligence and patience, and make labour agreeable or eligible to mankind, must also

1. *System of Moral Philosophy*, I, 319–320.

tend to the publick good. . . . Now nothing can so effec-
tually excite men to constant patience and diligence in all
sorts of useful industry, as the hopes of future wealth,
ease, and pleasure to themselves, their offspring, and all
who are dear to them." [2]

Both for individuals and a society the only way, said Hutcheson, to achieve this desirable state of affairs is

> by securing to everyone the fruits of his own labours,
> that he may enjoy them, or dispose of them as he pleases.
> If they are not thus secured, one has no other motive to
> labour than the general affection to his kind, which is
> commonly much weaker than the narrower affections to
> our friends and relations. [3]

He was perfectly aware that "the most extensive affections" by themselves would not "engage a wise man to industry," but the reverse would be the case "if property
ensued upon it." He concluded by saying that "both the immediate feelings of our hearts, and the consideration of the
general interest, suggest this law of nature that each one
should have the free use and disposal of what he has acquired by his own labour." [4] It is this which is property and
which may be defined when it is unlimited, as "a right to the
fullest use of any goods, and to dispose of them as one
pleases." [5]

Such was Hutcheson's justification for property, and, together with a labor expended in productive purposes, he
regarded occupation as the only other original means of acquiring property.

> Thus the first impulses of nature towards supporting our-
> selves, or those who are dear to us, point out the right of
> the first occupant to such things as are fit for present use.
> The obstructing this innocent design must appear morally
> evil, as it is ill-natured to hinder any man to take his

2. *Ibid.*, pp. 320–321.
3. *Ibid.*, p. 321.
4. *Ibid.*, p. 322.
5. *Ibid.*

natural support from the things granted for this purpose
by God and nature, while others can otherways support
themselves. . . . These considerations establish the first
rule of property, that *things fit for present use the first
occupier should enjoy undisturbed.*[6]

But Hutcheson did not make the property right absolute,
for he refused to accept the occupation of land as an invari-
able right to ownership. He based his distinction upon the
following cogent reasons:

No person or society therefore can by mere occupation acquire such a right in a vast tract of land quite beyond their
power to cultivate, as shall exclude others who may want
work, or sustenance for their numerous hands. . . . Thus
it would be vain for a private man with his domesticks
to claim a property, upon the circumstance of his first
having discovered or arrived at it, in a country capable
of maintaining ten thousand families, and requiring so
many to cultivate it.[7]

Hutcheson was not in favor of policies designed to promote "communism," and he phrased his criticism in the following manner: "If the goods procured, or improved by
the industrious lye in common for the use of all, the worst
of men have the generous and industrious for their slaves." [8]
In the same paragraph he recorded his dislike of sloth.

Such as are capable of labour, and yet decline it, should
find no support in the labours of others. . . . The most
benevolent temper must decline supporting the slothful
in idleness, that their own necessities may force them to
contribute their part for the public good.[9]

He believed that a communistic system of life would be
tolerable only if certain conditions he put forward could be
satisfactorily fulfilled.

6. *Ibid.*, pp. 317–318.
7. *Ibid.*, p. 326.
8. *Ibid.*, p. 321.
9. *Ibid.*, pp. 321–322.

These reasons for property . . . would not hold if a wise political constitution could compel all men to bear their part in labour, and then make a wisely proportioned distribution of all that was acquired, according to the indigence, or merit of the citizens.[10]

But he believed that the general feeling of sympathy would override such a proposal, and in any case

Such constant vigilance too of magistrates, and such nice discernment of merit, as could ensure both an universal diligence, and a just and humane distribution, is not to be expected. . . . What magistrate can judge of the delicate ties of friendship, by which a fine spirit may be so attached to another as to bear all toils for him with joy? . . . And what plan of policy will ever satisfy men sufficiently as to the just treatment to be given themselves . . . if all is to depend on the pleasures of magistrates? . . . Must all men in private stations ever be treated as children, or fools? [11]

Finally, referring particularly to the Utopias outlined by Sir Thomas More and Plato, Hutcheson maintained that

the inconveniences arising from property which (they) endeavour to avoid by the schemes of community, are not so great as those which must ensue upon community; and most of them may be prevented where property is allowed with all its innocent pleasures, by a *censorial* power, and proper laws about education, testaments and succession.[12]

His attitude to "schemes of community" was to admit the theoretical possibility of their success, but to see that, in the practical working of their implications, they were bound to fail simply because they ran counter to ineradicable and unchanging sentiments in human nature.

David Hume's foundation for the rationale of the institution of property received a very different emphasis from Hutcheson's. In the *Enquiry Concerning the Principles of*

10. *Ibid.*, p. 322.
11. *Ibid.*, pp. 322–323.
12. *Ibid.*, p. 323.

Morals,[13] Hume forcefully stated his meaning of private property in the economic system.[14] He began Section III of the *Enquiry*, a chapter entitled "Of Justice," with the blunt, uncompromising statement that "public utility is the *sole* origin of justice (*i.e.* the law regarding property), and that reflections on the beneficial consequences of this virtue are the sole foundation of its merit." [15] He then proceeded to argue that property has no *raison d'être* in conditions of economic abundance, for it arises and obtains its sanction only from the scarcity of commodities which have been appropriated. To illustrate this view he assumed, first, that

> nature has bestowed on the human race such profuse *abundance* of all *external* conveniences, that, without any uncertainty in the event, without any care or industry on our part, every individual finds himself fully provided with whatever his most voracious appetites can want, or luxurious imagination wish or desire. . . . The perpetual clemency of the seasons renders useless all cloaths or covering: The raw herbage affords him the most delicious fare; the clear fountain, the richest beverage. No laborious occupation required: No tillage: No navigation. Music, poetry, and contemplation form his sole business: Conversation, mirth, and friendship his sole amusement.[16]

Then he concluded that in such Elysian conditions

> every other social virtue would flourish, and receive tenfold encrease; but the cautious, jealous virtue of justice would never once have been dreamed of. For what purpose make a partition of goods, where every one already has more than enough? Why give rise to property, where there cannot possibly be any injury? Why call this object *mine*, when, upon the seizing of it by another, I need but stretch out my hand to possess myself

---

13. *Essays Moral, Political and Literary*, II, 179 *et seq.*
14. See Lionel Robbins, *The Theory of Economic Policy* (London: Macmillan Co., Ltd.), 1952, pp. 49–55, for an excellent appreciation of Hume's theory of property.
15. *Essays*, II, 179.
16. *Ibid.*, pp. 179–180.

of what is equally valuable? Justice, in that case, being totally *USELESS*, would be an idle ceremonial.[17]

His second assumption postulated a state in which the usual scarcity of goods and services existed, but in which

the mind is so enlarged, and so replete with friendship and generosity, that every man has the utmost tenderness for every man, and feels no more concern for his own interest that for that of his fellows.[18]

In such a case he concluded that

the *USE* of justice would, in this case, be suspended . . . nor would the divisions and barriers of property have ever been thought of. The whole human race would form only one family; where all would lie in common, and be used freely, without regard to property.[19]

In other words, there would be no use for property.

Continuing his exposition, Hume examined his third assumption, wherein the conditions of the first are completely reversed, so that a state of dire scarcity prevails.

Suppose a society fall into such want of all common necessaries, that the utmost frugality and industry cannot preserve the greater number from perishing. . . . It will readily, I believe, be admitted, that the strict laws of justice are suspended, in such a pressing emergence, and give place to the stronger motives of necessity and self-preservation. . . . The *USE* and *TENDENCY* of that virtue (justice) is to procure happiness and security, . . . but where the society is ready to perish from extreme necessity, no greater evil can be dreaded from violence and injustice.[20]

Under these conditions all regard for property is destroyed. He also showed that in cases where a man falls into the hands of ruffians, and where a civilized nation is at war with a barbarous one, all regard for property is suspended.

17. *Ibid.*, p. 180.
18. *Ibid.*
19. *Ibid.*, p. 181.
20. *Ibid.*, p. 182.

Thus, in concluding his argument based on these three premises he reckoned that he had proved the statement that the sole justification of property rests on utility. "By rendering justice totally *useless*, you thereby totally destroy its essence, and suspend its obligations upon mankind." [21]

Part II of his essay on *Justice* opened with a discussion of how property should be distributed. He postulated the existence of "a creature, possessed of reason, but unacquainted with human nature," with the task of framing rules of property which would best establish and promote public interest, peace, and security among mankind. Such a creature might "assign the largest possessions to the most extensive virtue," but Hume believed that only in a perfect theocracy, where an infinitely intelligent being governed, would such a rule serve the best purpose.

> But were mankind to execute such a law; so great is the uncertainty of merit, both from its natural obscurity, and from the self-conceit of each individual, that no determinate rule of conduct would ever result from it; and the total dissolution of society must be the immediate consequence.[22]

Hume is much more interested in the principle of equality and is of the opinion that "nature is so liberal to mankind, that, were all her presents equally divided among the species, and improved by art and industry, every individual would enjoy all the necessaries, and even most of the comforts of life." He believed that "wherever we depart from this equality, we rob the poor of more satisfaction than we add to the rich." [23]

Although he held these views about egalitarian distribution, he was convinced that its implementation was impracticable.

21. *Ibid.*, p. 183.
22. *Ibid.*, p. 187.
23. *Ibid.*, p. 188.

Historians, and even common-sense, may inform us, that, however specious these ideas of *perfect* equality may seem, they are really at bottom, *impracticable;* and were they not so, would be extremely *pernicious* to human society. Render possessions ever so equal, men's different degrees of art, care, and industry will immediately break that equality.[24]

He laid it down that

whatever is produced or improved by a man's art or industry ought, for ever, to be secured to him; . . . property ought also to descend to children and relations, for the same *useful* purpose . . . it may be alienated by consent, in order to beget that commerce and inter-course, which is so *beneficial* to human society . . . all contracts and promises ought carefully to be fulfilled, in order to secure mutual trust and confidence, by which the general *interest* of mankind is so much promoted.[25]

He then went on to claim that when writers on natural law were studied, it would be found that all of them, regardless of the principles they began with, would end by assigning

as the ultimate reason for every rule which they establish, the convenience and necessities of mankind. . . . What other reason, indeed, could writers ever give, why this must be *mine* and that *yours;* since uninstructed nature, surely, never made any such distinction. The objects which receive those appellations, are, of themselves, for-eign to us; they are totally disjoined and separated from us; and nothing but the general interests of society can form the connexion.[26]

At this point in his exposition, Hume went on to illustrate the artificiality of the law.

Sometimes, the interests of society may require a rule of justice in a particular case; but may not determine any particular rule among several, which are all equally bene-ficial. In that case, the slightest *analogies* are laid hold of,

24. *Ibid.*
25. *Ibid.*, p. 189.
26. *Ibid.*

in order to prevent that indifference and ambiguity, which would be the source of perpetual dissention. Thus possessions alone, and first possession, is supposed to convey property, where nobody else has any preceding claim and pretension. Many of the reasonings of lawyers are of this analogical nature, and depend on very slight connections of the imagination.[27]

Whenever a clash arises between public safety and interest and a private individual's interest, the private interest is sacrificed to the common interest, since the people's safety is the supreme law. He is well aware that on occasions the decision must be arbitrary, since

> sometimes both *utility* and *analogy* fail, and leave the laws of justice in total uncertainty. Thus, it is highly requisite, that prescription of long possession should convey property; but what number of days or months or years should be sufficient for that purpose, it is impossible for reason alone to determine.[28]

Therefore, as a general rule, all questions about property are determined by civil laws, which alter the rules of natural justice to conform with the particular convenience of each community. If a man's property is defined as anything which is lawful for him alone to use, and if it is asked what rule must be appealed to in order to dertermine such objects, Hume said:

> we must have recourse to statutes, customs, precedents, analogies, and a hundred other circumstances; some of which are constant and inflexible, some variable and arbitrary. But the ultimate point, in which they all professedly terminate, is, the interest and happiness of human society. Where this enters not into consideration, nothing can appear more whimsical, unnatural, and even superstitious, than all or most of the laws of justice and of property.[29]

27. *Ibid.*, pp. 189–190.
28. *Ibid.*, p. 190.
29. *Ibid.*, p. 191.

Hume's total disagreement with Hutcheson's exposition of
the origin of property is seen in the following comment:

> You sometimes, in my Opinion, ascribe the Original of
> Property and Justice to public Benevolence, and sometimes
> to private Benevolence towards the Possessors of the
> Goods, neither of which seem to me satisfactory. It morti-
> fies me much to see a Person, who possesses more Candour
> and Penetration than almost any I know, condemn Rea-
> sonings, of which I imagine I see so strongly the Evi-
> dence.[30]

Although it may seem a simple task to show that nature,
by means of an instinct, distinguishes property, in fact,

> there are required for that purpose ten thousand differ-
> ent instincts, and these employed about objects of the
> greatest intricacy, and nicest discernment. For when a
> definition of property is required, that relation is found
> to resolve itself into any possession acquired by occupa-
> tion, by industry, by prescription, by inheritance, by
> contract etc. Can we think, that nature, by an original
> instinct, instructs us all in these methods of acquisition?
>
> These words too, inheritance and contract, stand for
> ideas infinitely complicated; and to define them exactly,
> a hundred volumes of laws, and a thousand volumes of
> commentators, have not been found sufficient. Does na-
> ture, whose instincts in all men are simple, embrace such
> complicated and artificial objects, and create a rational
> creature, without trusting anything to the operation of his
> reason? [31]

Concluding his essay, Hume said that even if it were
granted that property could be distinguished by "a simple
original instinct," it would still not conform to the criteria of
a satisfactory definition of why property is justified, for

> is it by another original instinct, that we recognize the
> authority of kings and senates, and mark all the bound-
> aries of their jurisdiction? . . . Have we original innate

30. Extract of a letter, written in January, 1743, from Hume to Hutcheson.
Quoted from *The Letters of David Hume*, I, 47.
31. *Essays*, II, 194–195.

ideas of praetors and chancellors and juries? Who sees not, that all these institutions arise merely from the necessities of human society? [32]

In the same manner,

> the necessity of justice to the support of society is the *SOLE* foundation of that virtue; and since no moral excellence is more highly esteemed, we may conclude, that this circumstance of usefulness has, in general, the strongest energy, and most entire command over our sentiments. . . . As it also is the *SOLE* source of the moral approbation paid to fidelity, justice, veracity, integrity, and those other estimable and useful qualities and principles.[33]

Clearly, then, Hume regarded the institution of property as a necessary factor in the establishment of an orderly and well-organized state. In its absence, there would be a natural state of chaos and disorganization. Hume's attitude towards the "schemes of community" put forward from Plato onwards, or rather, towards that part of such schemes which advocated an egalitarian distribution of goods is summed up by his comment that "these ideas of *perfect* equality are really, at bottom, *impracticable*; and were they not so, would be extremely *pernicious* to human society." [34]

Hume, like Hutcheson, attempted no critical and systematic analysis of these Utopian schemes, but it is easy enough to detect in his work his feelings and attitudes towards these ideas. Basing his theory of property on utility, Hume argued that conditions could arise where it would become essential for the state to intervene, in order, for example, to resolve any disputes which might arise from the ownership of property. In such cases, utility dictated that the interests of the few individuals be subordinated to the interests of society as a whole.

32. *Ibid.*, p. 195.
33. *Ibid.*, p. 188.
34. *Ibid.*, p. 196.

Two neighbours may agree to drain a meadow, which they possess in common: because it is easy for them to know each other's mind; and each must perceive, that the immediate consequence of his failing in his part is the abandoning the whole project. But it is very difficult, and indeed impossible, that a thousand persons should agree in any such action; it being difficult for them to concert so complicated a design, and still more difficult for them to execute it. . . . Political society easily remedies both these inconveniences. Magistrates find an immediate interest in the interests of any considerable part of their subjects. They need consult nobody but themselves to form any scheme for the promoting of that interest. . . . Thus, bridges are built, harbours opened, ramparts raised, canals formed, fleets equipped, and armies disciplined, everywhere by the care of the government.[35]

Despite this important qualification, it was Hume's implicit assumption throughout his writing on this subject that private property is an integral part of the groundwork of economic life. Thus, it is a reasonable conclusion that Hume's insistence on private property implied a rejection of its opposite.

That this was his conclusion is illustrated by the following passage, where he depicts the difficulties of a state organized along the lines of ancient Sparta.

Could we convert a city into a kind of fortified camp, and infuse into each breast so martial a genius, and such a passion for public good, as to make everyone willing to undergo the greatest hardships for the sake of the public; these affections might now, as in ancient times prove alone a sufficient spur to industry, and support the community. It would then be advantageous, as in camps to banish all arts and luxury; and, by restrictions on equipage and tables, make the provisions and forage last longer than if the army were loaded with a number of superfluous retainers. But as these principles are too disinter-

35. *Ibid.*, II, 304.

ested and too difficult to support, it is requisite to govern
men by other passions, and animate them with a spirit
of avarice and industry, art and luxury. The camp is, in
this case, loaded with a superfluous retinue; but the provisions flow in proportionably larger. The harmony of
the whole is still supported; and the natural bent of the
minds being more complied with, individuals, as well as
the public, find their account in the observance of those
maxims.[36]

While Hume granted that a powerful argument could be
made out for schemes of equal distribution, he was quite
explicit and definite in rejecting this point of view. Nevertheless, he was by no means indifferent to the degree of
inequality which existed within the confines of a state, as
the following passage shows.

It will not, I hope, be considered as a superfluous digres-
sion, if I here observe, that, as the multitude of mechanical
arts is advantageous, so is the great number of persons,
to whose share the productions of these arts fall. A too
great disproportion among the citizens weakens any state.
Every person, if possible, ought to enjoy the fruits of his
labour, in a full possession of all the necessaries, and many
of the conveniences of life. No one can doubt, but such
an equality is most suitable to human nature, and diminishes much less from the *happiness* of the rich than it
adds to that of the poor. . . . When the riches are en-
grossed by a few, these must contribute very largely to
the supplying of the public necessities. But when the
riches are dispersed among multitudes, the burden feels
light on every shoulder. . . . Add to this that, where the
riches are in few hands, these must enjoy all the power,
and will readily conspire to lay the whole burden on the
poor, and oppress them still farther, to the discourage-
ment of all industry.[37]

In contrast to Hume's superb treatment of the theory of
property, references to this subject are difficult to find in the

36. *Ibid.*, I, 294–295.
37. *Ibid.*, pp. 296–297.

economic writings of Adam Smith. Part I, Division III, Sections 1-5, of Smith's 1763 *Lectures*, lists five legal ways in
which property may be acquired. This formalistic approach
is in marked contrast to both Hutcheson's and Hume's earlier philosophic speculations.

> Property is acquired five ways. First, by occupation, or
> the taking possession of what formerly belonged to no-
> body. Second, by accession, when a man has a right to one
> thing in consequence of another, as of a horse's shoe along
> with the horse. Third, by prescription, which is a right
> to a thing belonging to another arising from a long and
> uninterrupted possession. Fourth, by succession to our an-
> cestors or any other person, whether by a will or without
> one. Fifth, by voluntary transference, when one man de-
> livers over his right to another.[38]

This quotation and the ensuing twenty pages of the *Lectures* contain all of Smith's earlier views on property. No
philosophical consideration was attempted. He was merely
concerned with explaining the civil law in relation to the
five ways of acquiring property.

Smith made his first direct reference to property in the
Wealth of Nations in Book I, Chapter VI. In describing the
state of nature which "preceded both the accumulation of
stock and the appropriation of land," he maintained that
goods were exchanged for each other, according to "the proportions between the quantities of labour necessary for acquiring different objects." [39] In this early primitive state of
society "the whole produce of labour belongs to the labourer." [40] But

> As soon as the land of any country has all become private
> property, the landlords, like all other men, love to reap
> where they never sowed, and demand a rent even for its
> natural produce. The wood of the forest, the grass of the
> field, and all the natural fruits of the earth, which, when

38. *Lectures of Adam Smith*, p. 107.
39. *The Wealth of Nations*, I, 49.
40. *Ibid.*, p. 66.

land was in common, cost the labourer only the trouble of gathering them, come, even to him, to have an additional price fixed upon them.[41]

Smith's belief "that the whole produce of labour belongs to the labourer," which he restated on no less than five occasions, was of tremendous significance to the later development of theoretical socialism.[42] Long before Smith had written, John Locke had given a clear formulation of this doctrine:

> Every man has a property in his own person; this nobody has any right to but himself. The labour of his body, and the work of his hands, we may say, are properly his. Whatsoever then he removes out of the state that nature hath provided, and left it in, he hath mixed his labour with, and joined to it something that is his own, and thereby makes it his property.[43]

The direct relationship, however, between property and the development of civil government was a facet of the subject which Smith specifically mentioned.

> Among nations of hunters, as there is scarce any property, or at least none that exceeds the value of two or three day's labour; so there is seldom any established magistrate or any regular administration of justice. Men who have no property can injure one another only in their persons or reputations. . . . Avarice and ambition in the rich, in the poor the hatred of labour and the love of present ease and enjoyment, are the passions which prompt to invade property. . . . Wherever there is great property, there is great inequality. For one very rich man, there may be at least five hundred poor, and the affluence of the few supposes the indigence of the many. The affluence of the rich excites the indignation of the poor, who are often both driven by want, and prompted to envy, to invade his possessions. It is only under the shelter of civil magis-

41. *Ibid.*, p. 51.
42. *Ibid.*, pp. 67 and 68.
43. John Locke, *Essay concerning the true Original, Extent, and End of Civil Government*, Reprinted in *The Works of John Locke* (London: Printed by C. Baldwin, 1824), IV, 353–354.

trate that the owner of that valuable property . . . can sleep a single night in security. . . . The acquisition of valuable and extensive property, therefore, necessarily requires the establishment of civil government. Where there is no property, or at least none that exceeds the value of two or three days labour, civil government is not so necessary.[44]

Smith's insistence that "every man has a right to the produce of his own labour"—a view taken over from Hutcheson and Hume—is the foundation of property in the *Wealth of Nations.* "The property which every man has in his own labour, as it is the original foundation of all other property, so it is the most sacred and inviolable." [45]

Such then, as far as it goes, is Smith's treatment of the institution of property in the *Wealth of Nations.* Plainly, it is markedly inferior to the excellent analysis developed by Hume, and not as detailed or explicit as Hutcheson's. In the *Lectures* Smith's treatment of the subject was different from that in the *Wealth of Nations.* As has been shown, the former work lists five ways in which property may be acquired, but no mention is made of "the sacred and inviolable property which every man has in his own labour." Hutcheson maintained that "the right of property that each one has in the fruits of his own labour" is grounded in the general sympathy of mankind. Hume stated that public utility is the origin of property; but Smith merely laid down Hutcheson's statement of the subject, without any real justification of his own. In incorporating Locke's views on property, Smith granted that Locke's view of the matter was correct when applied to "the early and rude state of society." But, argued Smith, as soon as land is appropriated and, therefore, becomes a scarce good—together with the effect of payments made to the laborers by those who have accumulated stock—labor no longer receives all the fruits of

44. *Wealth of Nations,* II, 202–203.
45. *Ibid.,* I, 123.

its exertion. Land and capital, in this more advanced condition of society, also become economic goods and command a price. But this kind of analysis was not a justification of property. Smith advanced no theory about the origin of property; he simply recognized that private property belonged to the relatively few in society, and he implicitly assumed its inevitability.

Smith's attitude to "schemes of community" is as difficult to isolate in his work as is the theory of the origin of property. His attitude to this particular aspect of property cannot be ascertained with any exact degree of finality. There are two references in the *Wealth of Nations* to More's *Utopia* and Harrington's *Oceana*, but these are mainly criticisms of them as being unlikely developments of society, and not direct criticisms of any communistic features in these prescriptions.

> Such a speculation [how far the British system of taxation might be applicable to the Colonial Empire] can at worst be regarded but as a new Utopia, less amusing certainly, but not more useless and chimerical than the old one.[46]

And again:

> To expect, indeed, that the freedom of trade should ever be entirely restored in Great Britain, is as absurd as to expect that an Oceana or Utopia should ever be established in it.[47]

Nevertheless these views must be interpreted as negative criticisms of communistic ideals. A much better idea, however, of Smith's attitude to such idealistic schemes may be inferred from his searching critique of the "Mercantile System." His scathing and pungent denunciation of "mercantilism" may well be taken, indirectly, as representative of his opinion about "schemes of community."

One of Smith's chief criticisms of the "Mercantile System"

46. *Ibid.*, II, 419.
47. *Ibid.*, I, 435.

was that it caused a serious maldistribution of the economic resources of a country. It is, perhaps, plausible to assume that Smith would have applied the argument revolving round the maldistribution of resources to any of the "schemes of community." It was one of his chief charges against the "Mercantile System" that it was incompetent to control the manifold economic activities of citizens by central direction. Smith's strong disapproval of centrally controlled economic activity is admirably expressed in the following quotation.

> What is the species of domestic industry which his capital can employ, and of which the produce is likely to be of the greatest value, every individual, it is evident, can, in his local situation, judge much better than any statesman or lawgiver can do for him. The statesman, who should attempt to direct private people in what manner they ought to employ their capitals, would not only load himself with a most unnecessary attention, but assume an authority which could safely be trusted, not only to no single person, but to no council or senate whatever, and which would nowhere be so dangerous as in the hands of a man who had folly and presumption enough to fancy himself fit to exercise it.[48]

Further on in the *Wealth of Nations,* Smith reiterated this view:

> Every man, as long as he does not violate the laws of justice, is left perfectly free to pursue his own interest his own way, and to bring both his industry and capital into competition with that of any other man, or order of men. The sovereign is completely discharged from a duty, in the attempting to perform which he must always be exposed to innumerable delusions, and for the proper performance of which no human wisdom or knowledge could ever be sufficient; the duty of superintending the industry of private people, and of directing it towards the employments most suitable to the interest of the society.[49]

48. *Ibid.*, p. 421.
49. *Ibid.*, II, 184.

In 1759 Smith had expressed the same point of view in a more pungent and powerful passage in the *Theory of Moral Sentiments.*

> The man whose public spirit is promoted altogether by humanity and benevolence, will respect the established powers and privileges even of individuals, and still more those of the great orders and societies into which the state is divided. . . . The man of system, on the contrary, is apt to be very wise in his own conceit, and is often so enamoured with the supposed beauty of his own ideal plan of government, that he cannot suffer the smallest deviation from any part of it. He goes on to establish it completely and in all its parts, without any regard either to the great interests or to the strong prejudices which may oppose it: he seems to imagine that he can arrange the different members of a great society with as much ease as the hand arranges the different pieces upon a chess-board; he does not consider that the pieces upon the chess-board have no other principle of motion besides that which the hand impresses upon them; but that, in the great chess-board of human society, every single piece has a principle of motion of its own, altogether different from that which the legislature might choose to impress upon it. If those two principles coincide and act in the same direction, the game of human society will go on easily and harmoniously, and is very likely to be happy and successful. If they are opposite or different, the game will go on miserably, and the society must be at all times in the highest degree of disorder.[50]

Thus, Smith, like Hutcheson and Hume, was firmly opposed to any plan for the organization of society which involved the control, by central authorities, of the economic activity of individuals. In this respect, at least, Smith had absorbed the discussions about the theory of property contained in the works of his two eminent predecessors.

50. *The Theory of Moral Sentiments* (Edinburgh: John D. Lowe, 1849), pp. 342–343.

CHAPTER VIII

CONCLUDING COMMENTS

1

Why call me sage? The title sits better on my old teacher, the never-to-be-forgotten Dr. Hutcheson, as I called him on leaving Glasgow." [1]

By general consent in Anglo-Saxon countries Adam Smith is usually but mistakenly regarded as the originator of modern economics. The ordinary student of the general subject is largely content to trace the fascinating development of economics from Smith's contributions to the discipline. Certainly it is true that as a complete system of logical economic propositions, distinguished by balanced judgment, a mastery of descriptive economics, and magnificent interpretative powers, the *Wealth of Nations* stands head and shoulders above any rival expositions by Smith's contemporaries or predecessors. The justifiably unique position it occupies today in doctrinal history is proof of its stature. Nevertheless, many French and Italian writers about matters relating to political economy foreshadowed by way of pregnant suggestions and anticipations several fundamental elements in the Smithian exegesis. While it is, perhaps, an insoluble literary problem—but one of no little interest—to determine to what extent Smith's predecessors contributed to the definitive version of his political economy as set forth

1. Adam Smith, as quoted in James Bonar, *The Tables Turned* (London: Macmillan & Co., Ltd., 1931), p. 23.

in the *Wealth of Nations,* it is still possible to examine smaller parts of this field.

In particular, Francis Hutcheson and David Hume expressed some economic ideas with extraordinary acuteness, and often with a much keener awareness of their significance for the discipline as a whole, than did Adam Smith. The previous chapters have been concerned with isolating and studying cases of this kind. To discriminate precisely, however, wherein lies the undoubted superiority of Smith's work over that of his predecessors and contemporaries, when it is reviewed as a whole, is outside the framework of this book. In any case, this task has been performed much more adequately elsewhere.[2]

It was Adam Smith's good fortune to have as his inspiring teacher Francis Hutcheson, one of the foremost spirits of the Scottish Enlightenment, and to be blessed with the cherished friendship of David Hume, man of letters and perhaps the greatest of British philosophers. The economic sections of the works of these two men are studded with accurate and ingenious economic remarks. Often a study of these leads to the conclusion that they are the source of several of Adam Smith's fundamental economic contributions. Indeed, in some instances, notably in regard to Hutcheson's notions of the importance of scarcity and utility for a fundamental explanation of the theory of value, and Hume's analysis of money and interest, they are superior to Smith's own views of these subjects.

Much of the content of Adam Smith's economic analysis can be traced directly to Hutcheson. Although Smith was the first person to develop fully the wider economic signifi-

2. See particularly J. A. Schumpeter, *History of Economic Analysis* (London: George Allen & Unwin Ltd., 1954), pp. 181–194, which, although generally hostile to Smith's work, introduces new points of view. See also William Letwin, *The Origins of Scientific Economics* (London: Methuen and Co., Ltd., 1963), pp. 207–228; J. Cropsey, *Polity and Economy: An Interpretation of the Principles of Adam Smith* (The Hague: Martinus Nijhoff, 1957).

cance of the division of labor, he rested his exposition on Hutcheson's earlier statement of the matter; Smith recovered, rather than discovered, this concept. It was undoubtedly Hutcheson's lectures on the topic at Glasgow University which first directed Smith's attention to the economic importance of the subject. The superiority of Smith's understanding of the principle lies in its integration with the groundwork of his economic system.

Smith's economic analysis was designed to point to what he considered the fundamental factors leading to an economy's wealth, or "opulence." Hence, production was a matter of prime concern to him. Perhaps it was for this reason that Smith made no significant contribution to the theory of value, assuming that his preoccupation with labor and cost-of-production theories of value were divagations from the main path of analysis. In the 1763 *Lectures* Hutcheson's influence on Smith's value ideas is readily apparent. *Utility* and *scarcity* are given due recognition, as being basically essential to a satisfactory explanation of value. By 1776, however, Smith had unaccountably rejected the rich legacy which he had inherited through Hutcheson, and replaced it with his labor and cost-of-production theories of value.

Hutcheson was also the source of Smith's ideas on money. While Smith's treatment is more systematic than Hutcheson's, it is similar to it, especially in the discussion of the physical properties of money. Of the three writers, David Hume produced the most original work, with the most far-reaching consequences for subsequent monetary analysis. His discussion is the germ from which all the different types of modern dynamic monetary theories have evolved. Regrettably, Smith did not follow up the Humean contributions, making no attempt to employ Hume's brilliant analysis of the short run and the long run. He accepted the comparatively arid analysis of Hutcheson, and repeated it with scarcely any embellishments. He was seemingly unaware of the inherent excellence of Hume's monetary analysis.

Similarly, Hume's exposition of the rate of interest is superior to that of Hutcheson or Smith. Hutcheson tended to emphasize that the rate of interest depended only on the demand for, and the supply of, money. Hume, on the other hand, in an extensive and penetrating analysis of uniform excellence and perspicuity, cogently argued that the determination of the rate of interest depended mainly on the factors lying behind the aggregate volumes of lending and borrowing. He rejected the unsophisticated notion that interest was dependent on the quantity of money. Smith saw merit in the work of both Hutcheson and Hume. He accepted the view that interest was not dependent on the quantity of money, and he adopted the Humean technique of emphasizing the "real" factors behind the demand and supply aggregates. Although Smith's theory of interest owes more to Hume than to Hutcheson, his demand-and-supply analysis, together with his idea of the competition for scarce amounts of capital, may have stemmed from Hutcheson.

Hutcheson's uncompromising opposition, both on moral and economic grounds, to the Mandevillian thesis of the beneficence of expenditure on home-produced luxuries is probably the source of Smith's opposition to the doctrine. Although Hume was opposed on moral grounds to the doctrine, he realized that its economic implications were of great importance. Smith followed Hutcheson in denying that aggregate demand could be too low, and he trenchantly criticized luxury expenditure and praised the virtues of public and private parsimony.

Although Hutcheson supported the payments of bounties to infant industries and for imports of raw materials, he approached international trade essentially with a liberal point of view. His teaching in this respect was probably the first introduction that Smith had to the nature of liberal trade doctrines. David Hume, however, is the great name in this field. Like Hutcheson, he was not an outright free trader, for he approved of taxes on German linen and foreign brandy, but these were exceptions to his general policy. While Hume was undoubtedly a major source of Smith's free-trade views, care must be exercised in claiming too much for his influence on Smith. Hume did not publish his *Political Discourses* until 1752. On the other hand, in 1755 Smith went to considerable length to establish his prior claim to the originality of the principle of laissez-faire, expounded in his 1749 lectures at Edinburgh. In this respect Smith is probably indebted more to Hutcheson than to Hume, since there is scarcely an explicit hint of the laissez-faire notion in Hume's *Political Discourses,* while it is imbedded in the heart of all Hutcheson's economic writings.

Using all the stylistic devices of sarcasm and ridicule at his command, Hume in the *Political Discourses* effectively challenged the supposed merits of "mercantilist" trade policy and theory. It seems reasonably certain that Smith was guided by Hume's scathing attack when developing his only equally effective polemical assault on "mercantilist" shibboleths. It is all the more strange, therefore, that Smith in the *Wealth of Nations* did not attempt to incorporate in his argument against the "mercantilist" trade doctrines, Hume's most valuable analysis of the self-regulating adjustment of the specie-flow mechanism, even though he had approved of it in the *Lectures.*

In the field of taxation both Hume and Hutcheson contributed a great deal to Smith's statement of the four maxims of taxation. While certainty of the tax is the only maxim not stated by Hutcheson, Hume's discussion contains hints of each maxim. Although Hutcheson's discussion is brief, it is remarkably anticipatory of Smith's work. Hume's exposition, on the other hand, is considerably more detailed and thorough and equally anticipatory. It seems clear that these two writers guided Smith's thoughts in the field and enabled him to frame and develop as definite maxims the ideas and hints which had been so admirably presaged in their respective works.

Hume's discussion of the theory of property has been aptly praised as "one of the high points of speculative achievements in the sphere of moral science."[3] Hutcheson's treatment of the topic is also worthy of considerable commendation, especially his criticism of "schemes of community." But this was a subject with which Smith was not greatly concerned. He showed no sign of being interested in the origin or justification of property and did no more than comment that in the state of nature "the whole produce of labour belongs to the labourer," a conclusion to be found also in Hutcheson and Hume. He implicitly assumed the inevitability of private property, and, unlike Hutcheson and Hume, gave no explicitly detailed criticism of "schemes of community."

2

> It has already been shown that Hutcheson's work had made a great impression upon Smith and so it might have been conjectured that he would have availed himself of such material as proved suitable directly. Not only so, but in certain directions Hutcheson in Economics is closer than Hume to Adam Smith—in fact many of the principles used by both the later thinkers are traceable to the earlier one.[4]

This study of Francis Hutcheson and David Hume as predecessors of Adam Smith renders necessary a revaluation of Hutcheson and Hume's historical position and

3. L. C. Robbins, *The Theory of Economic Policy* (London: Macmillan & Co., Ltd., 1952), p. 50.
4. Scott, *Francis Hutcheson, His Life, Teaching and Position in the History of Philosophy*, pp. 233–234.

influence in the development and history of economic doctrines. Many of the salient features of Adam Smith's economic analysis were outlined and taught by Francis Hutcheson to Smith during his undergraduate days. Hutcheson's works contain the seeds of Smith's treatment of the division of labor, his concept of natural liberty, the basic outline of his theory of interest, his disapproval of luxury consumption, and three of his four maxims of taxation. So similar is the economic content of the *Lectures* of 1763 to Hutcheson's discussion of economic matters that they may well be described as an extended and sparkling, yet approving, commentary on Hutcheson's fundamental ideas. Chronologically considered, the content of Hutcheson's economic thought is of first-rate importance, since much of it is the genesis of major sections of Smith's economic system.

The influence of David Hume on Adam Smith is subsequent to the teachings of Francis Hutcheson. It would seem certain that the power and originality of Hume's delightfully urbane expositions confirmed Smith in the essential soundness of many of the economic concepts discussed by his beloved teacher. Hume's original contributions to economic thought lie in the fields of money, interest, and international trade and the theory of property. Smith went out of his way to acknowledge Hume's priority in relation to interest and money, but he failed to include in the framework of his analysis the more significant Humean contributions in this regard.

Hutcheson prepared the way for Hume and Smith, for without his pioneering teaching and discussions the dissemination and general acceptance of their ideas would have taken much longer. Preceding Hume and Smith, Hutcheson's work is worthy of the highest possible praise. While his influence is dominant in Smith's economics, Hume's *Political Discourses*, which also preceded Smith's major work, was pivotal in the construction of Smith's economic system and, just as important, helped to prepare a suitable climate of opinion for the propagation and reception of Smith's work.

After full weight has been given to the many excellent anticipations of Hutcheson and Hume, however, Smith must still receive homage as "the great master of our fellowship." [5] It was the originality of his genius that converted the pregnant hints and suggestions of his predecessors into a more logical economic system and mapped the contours of a new science.

> Sleep thou, O Father; resting on great deeds done, sure that to generations unborn they will be as beacons along the highways of history. Though thou art gone, may thy spirit, which so long moved the heart of things, inspire us to greater, nobler things.[6]

5. H. M. Robertson, *The Adam Smith Tradition* (Cape Town: University of Cape Town Press, 1950), p. 3.
6. Maori lament for R. J. Seddon, Prime Minister of New Zealand, 1893–1906.

SELECT BIBLIOGRAPHY
AND INDEX

SELECT BIBLIOGRAPHY

*The following list is restricted to the major works
cited in the text or footnotes. The original sources
of all quotations used in the text or footnotes are
given in the notes.*

BÖHM-BAWERK, EUGEN VON. *Capital and Interest: History and
Critique of Interest Theories.* Translated by George D.
Huncke and Hans F. Sennholz. Illinois: Libertarian Press,
1959. 3 vols.

―――――. *The Positive Theory of Capital.* Translated with a
Preface and Analysis by William Smart. London and New
York: Macmillan and Co., 1891.

BONAR, JAMES. "Adam Smith's Library," *The Economic Journal,*
XLVI (March, 1936).

―――――. *A Catalogue of the Library of Adam Smith.* 2nd ed.
London: Macmillan and Co., 1932.

―――――. *Philosophy and Political Economy in Some of Their
Historical Relations.* 3rd ed. London: George Allen & Unwin
Ltd., 1922.

―――――. *The Tables Turned.* London: Macmillan and Co., 1931.

BRYSON, GLADYS. *Man and Society: The Scottish Inquiry of the
Eighteenth Century.* Princeton, New Jersey: Princeton University Press, 1945.

CANNAN, EDWIN. *A Review of Economic Theory.* London: P. S.
King & Son, 1929.

CANTILLON, RICHARD. *Essai sur la nature du commerce en général.* Ed. Henry Higgs. London: Frank Cass & Co. Ltd., 1959.

CARMICHAEL, GERSHOM. *De Officio.* 2nd ed. Edinburgh: R. and
A. Foulis, 1724.

CROPSEY, JOSEPH. *Polity and Economy: An Interpretation of the Principles of Adam Smith.* ("International Scholars Forum," No. 8.) The Hague: Martinus Nijhoff, 1957.

The Defects of an University Education. London, 1772.

FAY, C. R. *Adam Smith and the Scotland of His Day.* ("Publication of the Department of Social and Economic Research, University of Glasgow, Social and Economic Studies," No. 3.) Cambridge: At the University Press, 1956.

———. *The World of Adam Smith.* Cambridge: W. Heffer & Sons, Ltd., 1960.

FURNISS, EDGAR S. *The Position of the Laborer in a System of Nationalism: A Study in the Labor Theories of the Later English Mercantilists.* ("Reprints of Economic Classics.") New York: Kelley & Millman, Inc., 1957.

HIRST, F. W. *Adam Smith.* London: Macmillan and Co., 1904.

HUME, DAVID. *Essays Moral, Political and Literary.* Eds. T. H. Green and T. H. Grose. London: Longmans, Green, and Co., 1875. 2 vols.

———. *Letters of David Hume.* Ed. J. V. T. Greig. Oxford: The Clarendon Press, 1932.

———. *Life and Correspondence of David Hume.* Ed. John Hill Burton. Edinburgh: William Trail, 1846. 2 vols.

———. *Writings on Economics.* Ed. Eugene Rotwein. Edinburgh: Nelson, 1953.

HUTCHESON, FRANCIS. *Introduction to Moral Philosophy.* 2nd ed. Glasgow: Printed and Sold by Robert and Andrew Foulis, Printers to the University, 1753.

———. *Reflections upon Laughter and Remarks upon the Fable of the Bees.* Glasgow: R. and A. Foulis, 1750.

———. *A System of Moral Philosophy in Three Books. To which is prefixed some account of the Life, Writings, and Character of the Author by the Reverend William Leechman.* Glasgow: R. and A. Foulis, 1755.

HUTCHISON, T. W. "Berkeley's *Querist* and Its Place in the Economic Thought of the Eighteenth Century," *The British Journal for the Philosophy of Science,* IV (May, 1953), 52–77.

JOHNSON, E. A. J. *Predecessors of Adam Smith: The Growth of British Political Thought.* ("Prentice-Hall Economics Series.") New York: Prentice-Hall Inc., 1937.

KEYNES, J. M. "Adam Smith as Student and Professor," *Economic History,* III (February, 1938), 33–46.

————. *The General Theory of Employment Interest and Money*. London: Macmillan and Co., 1936.

———— AND SRAFFA, P. *An Abstract of a Treatise of Human Nature, 1740: A Pamphlet Hitherto Unknown by David Hume*. Cambridge: The University Press, 1938.

LASKI, H. J. *Political Thought in England from Locke to Bentham*. London: Oxford University Press, 1920.

LETWIN, WILLIAM. *The Origins of Scientific Economics*. London: Methuen & Co. Ltd., 1963.

LOCKE, JOHN. *Essay Concerning the True Original, Extent, and End of Civil Government*. Reprinted in the *Works of John Locke*. London: C. Baldwin, 1824. 9 vols.

London Critical Review, XXV, December, 1795.

MANDEVILLE, BERNARD DE. *The Fable of the Bees*. Ed. F. B. Kaye. Oxford: Clarendon Press, 1924. 2 vols.

McCOSH, JAMES. *The Scottish Philosophy, Biographical, Expository, Critical: From Hutcheson to Hamilton*. London: Macmillan and Co., 1875.

MONROE, ARTHUR ELI (ed.). *Early Economic Thought: Selections from Economic Literature Prior to Adam Smith*. Cambridge, Mass.: Harvard University Press, 1951.

MOSSNER, ERNEST CAMPBELL. *The Life of David Hume*. Edinburgh: Nelson, 1954.

MURRAY, DAVID. *Memories of the Old College of Glasgow*. ("Glasgow University Publications," No. III.) Glasgow: Jackson, Wylie and Co., 1927.

PETTY, SIR WILLIAM. "Political Arithmetic," in George A. Aitken (ed.), *Later Stuart Tracts*. Westminster: Archibald Constable & Co. Ltd., 1903.

PUFENDORF, SAMUEL VON. *De Officio Hominis Et Civis Juxta Legem Naturalem Libri Duo*. Trans. Frank Gardner Moore, ed. James Brown Scott. New York: Oxford University Press, 1927. 2 vols.

RAE, JOHN. *Life of Adam Smith*. London: Macmillan and Co., 1895.

ROBBINS, LIONEL. *The Theory of Economic Policy in English Classical Political Economy*. London: Macmillan and Co., 1952.

ROBERTSON, H. M. *The Adam Smith Tradition*. ("An Inaugural Lecture.") Cape Town: University of Cape Town Press, 1950.

————— AND TAYLOR, W. L. "Adam Smith's Approach to the Theory of Value," *Economic Journal*, LXVII (June, 1957), 181–198.

SCHUMPETER, JOSEPH A. *History of Economic Analysis*. London: George Allen and Unwin, Ltd., 1954.

SCOTT, WILLIAM ROBERT. *Adam Smith as Student and Professor*. ("Glasgow University Publications," No. XLVI.) Glasgow: Jackson, Son & Company, 1937.

—————. *Francis Hutcheson: His Life, Teaching, and Position in the History of Philosophy*. Cambridge: Cambridge University Press, 1900.

—————. *Studies Relating to Adam Smith during the Last Fifty Years*. Ed. A. L. Macfie. Proceedings of the British Academy, Vol. XXVI. London: Humphrey Milford, 1962.

SEN, S. R. *The Economics of Sir James Steuart*. London: G. Bell and Sons Ltd., 1957.

SMITH, ADAM. *Lectures of Adam Smith*. Ed. Edwin Cannan. Oxford: Clarendon Press, 1896.

—————. *Lectures on Rhetoric and Belles Lettres*. Ed. John M. Lothian. London: Thomas Nelson and Sons Ltd., 1963.

—————. *The Theory of Moral Sentiments*. Edinburgh: John D. Lowe, 1849.

—————. *The Theory of Moral Sentiments with a Life of the Author*. London: 1822. 2 vols.

—————. *The Wealth of Nations*. Ed. Edwin Cannan. London: Methuen and Co., 1930. 2 vols.

SMITH, NORMAN KEMP. *The Philosophy of David Hume: A Critical Study of Its Origins and Central Doctrines*. Macmillan and Co., 1949.

STEUART, SIR JAMES. *An Inquiry into the Principles of Political Oeconomy*. London: A Millar and T. Caddell, 1767. 2 vols.

STEWART, DUGALD. *The Collected Works*. Ed. Sir William Hamilton. Edinburgh: T. Constable & Co., 1854. 10 vols.

TAYLOR, W. L. "A Short Life of Sir James Steuart: Political Economist," *The South African Journal of Economics*, XXV (September, 1957), 290–302.

—————. "Gershom Carmichael: A Neglected Figure in British Political Economy," *The South African Journal of Economics*, XXIII (September, 1955), 251–255.

TURGOT, ANNE ROBERT JACQUES. *Reflections on the Formation*

and the Distribution of Riches. ("Economic Classics Series.")
Ed. W. J. Ashley, New York: The Macmillan Company, 1898.
TYTLER, A. F. *Henry Home of Kames.* Edinburgh: 1807.
VINER, JACOB. *Studies in the Theory of International Trade. New*
York: Harper and Brothers, 1937.

INDEX